I0800834

IMAGES of America

CUMBERLAND GAP NATIONAL HISTORICAL PARK

This 19th-century print depicts a family's journey westward through the Cumberland Gap. The meadows with flowers and a flat, well-tended road lend a romantic flavor to the pioneer's story. The reality was often much more harsh. (Courtesy of the Cumberland Gap National Historical Park.)

ON THE COVER: A park ranger looks out over the scenery of the Cumberland Mountains and beyond from Wind Gap overlook in 1959. From this vantage point, the three states that make up the Cumberland Gap National Historical Park—Kentucky, Virginia, and Tennessee—can be seen. (Courtesy of the Cumberland Gap National Historical Park.)

IMAGES
of America

CUMBERLAND GAP NATIONAL HISTORICAL PARK

Martha Evans Wiley

ARCADIA
PUBLISHING

ISBN 978-1-4671-1111-9

Published by Arcadia Publishing
Charleston, South Carolina

Printed in the United States of America

Library of Congress Control Number: 2013939948

For all general information, please contact Arcadia Publishing:
Telephone 843-853-2070
Fax 843-853-0044
E-mail sales@arcadiapublishing.com
For customer service and orders:
Toll-Free 1-888-313-2665

Visit us on the Internet at www.arcadiapublishing.com

To Virginia Huff, whose commitment and love
for the park have inspired so many

Contents

Acknowledgments

I owe many thanks to the staff at Cumberland Gap National Historical Park for their help and patience over the months I have spent working on this book, and I am especially grateful to Carol Borneman for her diligent proofreading. I would also like to thank my family, especially my daughter Emma, for helping around the house while I was preoccupied. My husband offered both encouragement and editorial help. Lincoln Memorial University archivist Michelle Ganz was always quick to respond with a photograph when needed, and fellow author Natalie Sweet helped me stay on track. Arcadia acquisitions editor Liz Gurley was always available to answer any questions I had throughout the publishing process.

Unless otherwise noted, all images are courtesy of the Cumberland Gap National Historical Park archives. Images provided by the Abraham Lincoln Library and Museum, Lincoln Memorial University are abbreviated as (ALLM of LMU), and images courtesy of the Bell County, Kentucky Historical Society are abbreviated as (BCHS).

INTRODUCTION

A gap is sometimes defined as a break in a barrier, and for centuries, that is what Cumberland Gap meant to hundreds of thousands of people. It was a means to an end, a low point in a mountain range long viewed as an impediment to the expansion of the English colonies and, later, the nascent United States. It wasn't until the early 20th century that some began to see Cumberland Gap as a place important in its own right—a vital part of America's story that deserved to be recognized and preserved.

Encompassing more than 24,000 acres in Kentucky, Virginia, and Tennessee, Cumberland Gap National Historical Park contains some of the poorest and most rugged areas of Appalachia. The park was first conceived of in 1922 and authorized by Congress in 1940, but it wasn't formally dedicated until 1959. Since then, the park has seen many changes, both in identity and purpose.

While the Cumberland Gap is closely identified with such notable historical figures as Dr. Thomas Walker and Daniel Boone, there are scores of lesser-known stories associated with this unassuming pass through the Cumberland Mountain range. When Boone hacked his trace through the deep forest and began leading settlers west, the dam broke; more than 300,000 people followed his trace to the legendary bluegrass of Kentucky and beyond. Today, it is estimated that 48 million Americans can trace their ancestors to having traveled through the Cumberland Gap.

Local citizens first floated the idea of a national park at Cumberland Gap in the 1920s, wanting to protect the spectacular scenery from the mining and logging that was devastating the landscape. But the park was also the creation of a community of dreamers who saw the need to preserve and share the stories of Boone and the pioneers who traveled through the Gap on their way to a better life.

The journey of the park's creation was at times as rough as that of the westward-bound settlers. It took almost 20 years to pass the legislation necessary to authorize the park, reflecting some confusion as to the focus of what was to be the largest national historical park east of the Mississippi. World War II delayed land acquisition, as did the difficulty in tracking down hundreds of small landowners in the mountains of the three states to convince them to sell and establish boundaries. The park boundary was surveyed three times in the 1940s and 1950s to avoid later disputes.

The dedication of the park finally arrived on the weekend of July 3, 1959. Vice Pres. Richard M. Nixon presided over a parade that Middlesboro, Kentucky, residents still recall as the biggest day in their town's history. Thousands attended, and hundreds participated in the formal recognition of the newest national historical park.

After the dedication, the park grew quickly, both in program and facilities. The focus of the park's programming alternated between the cultural history within its boundaries and its incredible natural diversity. But the dream of a few back in the early days of the park was never forgotten, that of one day being able walk through the Cumberland Gap in the footsteps of Daniel Boone.

This dream took a step forward in 1973 when a law was passed directing the National Park Service (NPS) to build a twin-bore tunnel under Cumberland Mountain to divert traffic from the dangerous road over the gap. Progress toward this goal was slow at times but picked up once the actual work began. The grand opening of the state-of-the-art tunnel was held in October 1996 and, despite the rainy weather, was well attended by dignitaries and the public. As the procession of historical reenactors paraded by, making their way through this 21st-century marvel, the frontier disappeared and all barriers were surmountable.

Thus, the stage was set for the final step in the process, one that was set in motion decades before: the physical restoration of the Wilderness Road landscape over the Cumberland Gap. The new tunnel removed the vehicle traffic and made it possible to tear up the roughly 13,000 tons of asphalt of US Highway 25E—a road that had been in place in some form or another for almost a century—and restore the rough dirt trail of Boone's time. Research on this daunting project had been ongoing throughout tunnel construction. Working from an exhaustive study prepared by NPS historian Jere L. Krakow in 1987, NPS visual information specialist Michael F. Hart combined period maps and journals, extant road traces, historic and aerial photographs, and old-fashioned field work to guide the construction crews in recreating the trail of centuries earlier.

After nine months of rigorous work, the trail was completed in 2002, averaging 10 feet in width for a 1.2-mile stretch from Virginia to Kentucky, through the saddle of the Cumberland Gap. It was time for another dedication, this time celebrating the opening of the storied Wilderness Road, once again open for foot traffic. Again, the procession of history made its way through the Cumberland Gap, echoing the footsteps of those settlers from so long ago. In a more somber mood than felt in 1996, Native Americans, pioneers with their livestock and families, and long hunters retraced the journey of so many of America's forefathers, this time more aware of the harsh realities of the trek.

In his 1893 paper "The Significance of the Frontier in American History," historian Frederick Jackson Turner hypothesized that our country's history is one of overcoming a series of frontiers. By restoring even this small tangible link to America's early identity, it is now possible to once again, "Stand at Cumberland Gap and watch the procession of civilization, marching single file—the buffalo following the trail to the salt springs, the Indian, the fur-trader and hunter, the cattle-raiser, the pioneer farmer—and the frontier has passed by."

One

Westward Bound

Lay down boys an' take a little nap, fourteen miles to the Cumberland Gap.

—Henry H. Fuson, *Ballads of the Kentucky Highlands*

People have been traveling through the Cumberland Gap for centuries, following the well-established trails of the bison and deer as they wound their way through the rugged pass. They came for any number of reasons; some to seek their fortune, some for more elbow room, and some just out of curiosity. Called the "Gateway to the West," Cumberland Gap's role in the flow of goods and information back east has sometimes been overlooked. But it was the tales of discovery and the abundance of riches in the form of furs, minerals, and other wonders that fueled the dreams of people back home and kept them moving west.

The reasons for coming to Cumberland Gap changed in the 1860s, as armies of both North and South realized its strategic importance as a border between slave and neutral territory. Although the men involved in that conflict have gone, the scars from the devastation still appear on the land at the gap. Fortunes were made and broken here, as were allegiances that, by necessity, changed with the army of the moment.

As the 19th century progressed, more wonders were to be found beneath the surface of the Wilderness Road and the surrounding mountains. Iron ore and coal were discovered, riches that drew men from across the ocean, inspired to build a city exploiting this mineral wealth. With them came the railroad, an engineering marvel that made the crumbling road over the gap an anachronism, but only for a short time.

By the early 1900s, the advent of the automobile was changing the landscape of America forever. The old Wilderness Road over the Cumberland Gap was paved and once again became part of a system of roads that connected east, west, north, and south. People returned in droves to the gap, this time seeing the peaks and caves not as impediments or entities to be exploited, but as natural marvels to be explored and enjoyed.

Gateway to the West: Daniel Boone Leading the Settlers Through the Cumberland Gap, 1775 was painted by Kentucky native David Wright in 2000 and has been designated the official state Daniel Boone portrait. This carefully researched painting was commissioned for Cumberland Gap National Historical Park and adapted into a mural in the visitor center. (Courtesy of David Wright.)

David Wright painted this depiction of a Cherokee warrior from the 18th century. Both the Cherokee and the Shawnee used the Warriors Path through the Cumberland Gap as a trade route and, at times, a warpath. Projectile points and pieces of pottery found in rock shelters and near streams tell the story of these first Americans in the area. (Courtesy of David Wright.)

Both Meriwether Lewis and Capt. William Clark returned to Virginia from their Corps of Discovery exploration through the Cumberland Gap in 1806, although not together. Lewis, shown here in an 1805 engraving by Charles Balthazar Julien Févret de Saint-Mémin, took time at the gap to resurvey the boundary between Tennessee and Kentucky to settle a long-standing dispute. (Courtesy of the Library of Congress, LC-USZ62-105848.)

This drawing from the end of the 19th century depicts Daniel Boone defending his family from a Native American attack. While the legends that grew up around Boone after his death embellished his adventures, the threat of Indian attacks in the wilderness was very real: Boone lost two sons, James and Israel, to such attacks. (Courtesy of the Library of Congress, LC-DIG-ppmsca-23155.)

The rich iron ore and vast timber tracts in the southern Appalachians made the gap region attractive for early industrialists. This depiction by Harry Fenn, published in *Picturesque America* (1874), shows the iron furnace in the town of Cumberland Gap, Tennessee, in the shadow of the Pinnacle of Cumberland Mountain.

The iron furnace fell into disrepair during the Civil War and ceased operation for good in the 1870s. Owner John G. Newlee received a receipt from Union general George Morgan for the damage done to his property while occupied by Union troops in June 1862. Below, it is as it appeared just before the park acquired the property; the water wheel and other additions are long gone, and Gap Creek has cut new channels across the slag pile.

Built by Martin Beatty, the iron foundry business passed to John G. Newlee in the 1840s when he moved to the area. Census records show that Newlee owned a few slaves who worked at the furnace. Newlee's daughter Mary Adeline Newlee Devine (left) and sister Melissa "Mellie" Newlee (right) lived in Cumberland Gap as well. This tintype photograph was made about 1855.

This undated image from the late 19th century is one of the most evocative images of the lonely and wild road through the Cumberland Gap. These travelers are approaching the gap from the Kentucky side and illustrate the three modes of getting through the gap at that time: on foot, on horseback, and by wagon. Fog softens the rugged nature of the Pinnacle, seen to the left.

This very early image of a slightly different angle of the Cumberland Gap is believed to date from 1861. The absence of trees on the mountainsides indicates that the photograph dates after June, when the Confederate army occupied the gap. One of the soldiers' first jobs was to clear the forest to allow for better visibility and the building of fortifications; one of which, Fort McCook or "Rocky Fort," was located on the knoll in the center of this photograph. (Courtesy of ALLM of LMU.)

When the Civil War began in April 1861, the small Kentucky and Tennessee communities on either side of the Cumberland Gap were predominantly pro-Union in their sentiments. In this print, tents and fortifications can be seen in the town of Cumberland Gap in Tennessee. Note the smoke from fires set by retreating Union forces in September 1862 as they attempted to destroy their stores before the arrival of the Confederate army.

Harper's Weekly was the most widely read periodical in the country during the Civil War, and its woodcuts of events in all theaters of the war are collectors' items today. This September 1863 print shows the last significant action seen at the gap, when Union general Ambrose Burnside's troops moved in to take over Confederate general John W. Frazer's forces without a shot fired.

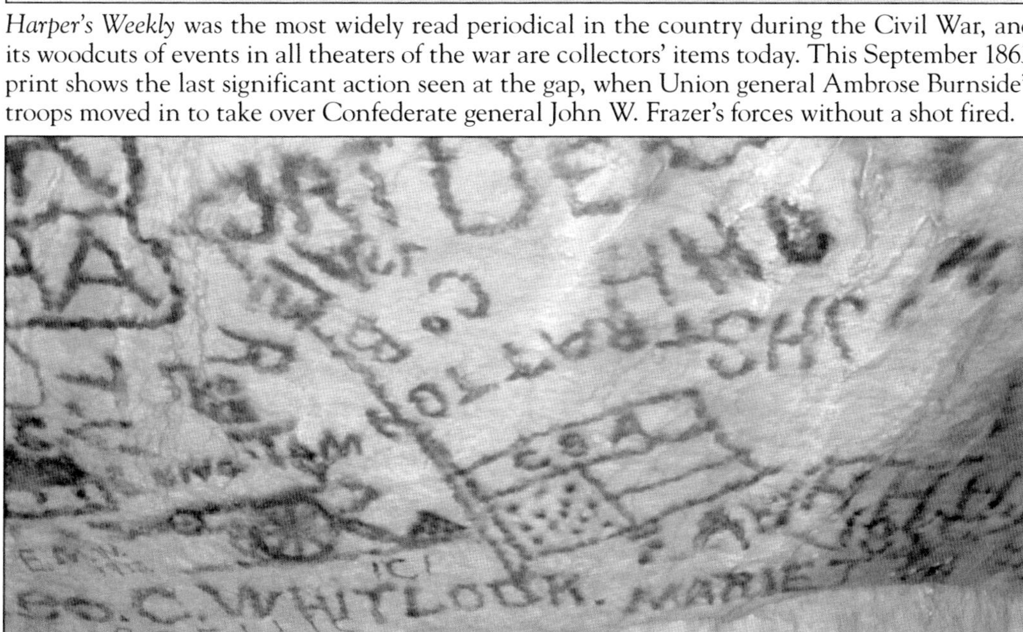

The soldiers stationed at the gap during the Civil War left more than their fortifications, roads, and rifle pits. This depiction of a Confederate flag and a legendary artillery piece dubbed "Long Tom" are just a fraction of the graffiti found inside Soldiers Cave today. Since 2003, the Cave Research Foundation has been mapping and documenting historical signatures in the cave, some dating as far back as 1814.

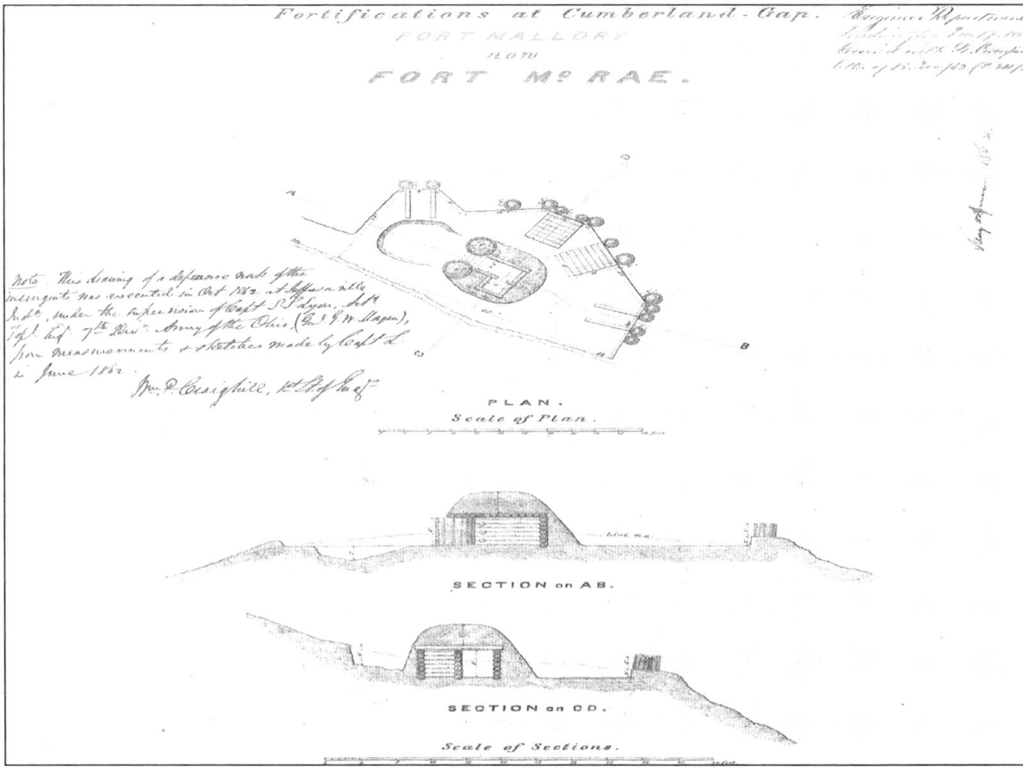

Fort McRae was destroyed by the building of the Skyland Road up the Pinnacle in the 1920s. This and several other earthworks in the park were built by the Confederate army in 1861 during their first occupation of the gap. In 1862, as the Union army moved in, the fort was improved upon, as shown in this sketch by Union army engineer William Craighill. The gap changed hands two more times during the war.

Union lieutenant colonel George W. Monroe served with Brig. Gen. George W. Morgan at Cumberland Gap during the summer of 1862. Capturing the gap from the Confederates in June, Morgan held the pass until September when he was forced to evacuate by Gen. Edmund Kirby Smith, blowing up all the stores as he and his men fled the approaching forces.

One of the more famous incidents of the Civil War occurred at Baptist Gap, east of Cumberland Gap. In August 1862, a Confederate regiment of Cherokee Indians, under the command of longtime friend and advocate William Holland Thomas, ambushed a number of Union soldiers in retaliation for the killing of their chief. (Courtesy of the Museum of the Cherokee Indian.)

Pvt. Samuel Truehart was one of the soldiers in the 5th Regiment Cavalry, US Colored Troops as they came through the Cumberland Gap on their way to the Battle of Saltville in December 1864. (Courtesy of David E. Brown, www. 5thuscc.net.)

This painting by private Archibald M. Willard of the 86th Ohio Volunteer Infantry is dated 1864, when the gap was fortified by a few Union troops. Interesting to note is the forested area right of center, denoting the Gap Creek and the location of a mill and iron furnace just behind. Willard did several sketches during his time at the Gap and later went on to paint the iconic *Spirit of '76*.

Titled "Spring Branch from King Solomon's Cave," this post–Civil War photograph is a perfect complement to the Willard painting. Gap Creek originated in Gap Cave, located directly above the industrial area, and powered waterwheels for both the woolen mill and the iron furnace. Today, the creek's waters are bottled by the Coca-Cola Company and sold in the local communities. (Courtesy of BCHS.)

These two late-19th-century photographs show the area recovering from the trauma of the Civil War. Above, the area shown deforested in the Willard painting has abundant new growth, and the Wilderness Road can no longer be seen clearly. Below, in an enlarged view of the saddle of the gap taken from the Kentucky side, the bridge spanning the gap between Forts Halleck and McClellan can be seen, as can the Harlan Road (lower center). Both forts were later destroyed by the widening of the road through the gap in the early 20th century.

In July 1875 and 1876, Harvard University and the Kentucky Geological Survey (KGS) held a summer field school at Cumberland Gap, dubbed Camp Harvard. The camp was situated on the site of an old Civil War fort, now known to be Fort McCook, judging from the photograph. Some of the students were veterans from that conflict of just 10 years earlier. (Courtesy of the University of Kentucky Special Collections, Albert R. Crandall Photograph Collection.)

Titled "Blighted Hopes—Nothing but Iron, Sir," this photograph illustrates an encounter between a mountain resident and one of the Harvard geologists. The encounters between the local residents of the gap and the visiting scholars from the north were described with humor in the students' journals. Here, a local prospector shows one of the students what he has found. Lexington-based photographer James Mullen was hired by the KGS to photograph daily life at the camp. (Courtesy of the UK Special Collections, Crandall Collection.)

The Harvard geologists discovered the incredible diversity of minerals abundant throughout the area of Cumberland Gap, and their finds were cited in studies promoting the potential for growth in the area based on the wealth of minerals and timber. Scottish developer Alexander Arthur used the information in his planning and promotion of the industrial city of Middlesboro, Kentucky, in 1889. Many of the students who studied at Cumberland Gap later went on to become leaders in their field, like John Proctor, the future director of the Kentucky Geological Survey. As can be seen from these two group photographs, some students and instructors brought their wives and children with them. (Both, courtesy of the UK Special Collections, Crandall Collection.)

The railroad came late to the Cumberland Gap area and was aggressively promoted by Scottish developer Alexander Arthur, a progressive thinker who predicted that his new industrial center of Middlesboro, Kentucky, and its resort companion town of Harrogate, Tennessee, would attract crowds of pleasure-seekers. Events conspired against him, however, including this accident during the 1889 inaugural train trip north along the Knoxville, Cumberland Gap & Louisville Railroad. (Courtesy of ALLM of LMU.)

The Four Seasons resort was the epitome of Gilded Age opulence, if somewhat out of place in the rugged Cumberland Mountains. Arthur hoped to attract celebrities and society's leaders to this 700-room hotel and spa complete with sanitarium (shown here), carriage trails, and wine cellars. Just three years after opening in 1892, however, the resort closed its doors, a victim of over-ambitious dreams and the financial panics of the 1890s. (Courtesy of ALLM of LMU.)

HOW TO REACH HARROGATE

(Cumberland Gap Park and Four Seasons Hotel)

FROM NORTH AND NORTHWEST VIA CHICAGO AND LOUISVILLE.

....	7.25 pm	Lv... MINNEAPOLIS... Ar	8.10 am	11.35 pm
....	8.05 pm	Lv........St. Paul........Ar	7.30 am	11.05 pm
4.00 pm	7.00 am	Lv......Milwaukee......Ar	8.30 pm	11.00 am
6.30 pm	9.30 am	Ar........Chicago........Lv	6.00 pm	8.30 am
11.50 pm	6.20 pm	Lv........Omaha........Ar	9.30 am	8.15 am
2.15 pm	9.30 am	Ar........Chicago........Lv	6.00 pm	12.00 n'n
8.20 pm	9.45 am	Lv........Chicago........Ar	5.25 pm	7.30 am
3.40 am	4.00 pm	Lv......Indianapolis......Ar	11.10 am	11.50 pm
7.10 am	7.40 pm	Ar.......Louisville.......Lv	7.31 am	7.35 pm
8.45 am	8.30 pm	Lv.......Louisville.......Ar	7.00 am	5.10 pm
7.20 pm	6.10 am	Ar....HARROGATE....Lv	9.25 pm	6.53 am

Sleeping cars through from St. Paul, Minneapolis and Omaha to Chicago, Chicago to Louisville and Louisville to Harrogate.

FROM NORTH AND NORTHWEST VIA CHICAGO AND CINCINNATI.

....	7.25 pm	Lv... MINNEAPOLIS... Ar	8.10 am	....
....	8.05 pm	Lv........St. Paul........Ar	7.30 am	....
....	7.00 am	Lv......Milwaukee......Ar	8.30 pm	....
....	9.30 am	Ar........Chicago........Lv	6.00 pm	....
....	6.20 pm	Lv........Omaha........Ar	9.30 am	....
....	9.30 am	Ar........Chicago........Lv	6.00 pm	....
....	9.45 am	Lv........Chicago........Ar	5.20 pm	....
....	3.00 pm	Lv......Indianapolis......Ar	11.25 am	....
....	7.00 pm	Ar......Cincinnati......Lv	8.05 am	....
....	7.30 pm	Lv......Cincinnati......Ar	7.20 am	....
....	6.10 am	Ar....HARROGATE....Lv	9.25 pm	....

Sleeping cars through from St. Paul, Minneapolis and Omaha to Chicago, Chicago to Cincinnati and Cincinnati to Harrogate.

FROM WEST AND NORTHWEST VIA ST. LOUIS AND LOUISVILLE.

7.00 pm	9.00 am	Lv... MINNEAPOLIS... Ar	6.35 pm	7.55 am
7.15 pm	9.15 am	Lv........St. Paul........Ar	6.30 pm	7.45 am
....	6.00 pm	Lv......Des Moines......Ar	9.00 am	....
6.15 pm	7.30 am	Ar.......St. Louis.......Lv	8.25 pm	9.00 am
9.45 pm	4.10 pm	Lv........Omaha........Ar	12.45 n'n	6.30 am
10.00 am	8.35 pm	Lv.....Kansas City.....Ar	7.00 am	6.00 pm
6.15 pm	7.30 am	Ar.......St. Louis.......Lv	8.25 pm	9.00 am
8.25 pm	8.20 am	Lv.......St. Louis.......Ar	6.55 pm	6.45 am
7.00 am	6.55 pm	Ar.......Louisville.......Lv	8.10 am	8.25 pm
8.45 am	8.30 pm	Lv.......Louisville.......Ar	7.00 am	5.10 pm
7.20 pm	6.10 am	Ar....HARROGATE....Lv	9.25 pm	6.53 am

Sleeping cars through from St. Paul, Minneapolis, Omaha and Kansas City to St. Louis, St. Louis to Louisville and Louisville to Harrogate.

FROM WEST AND NORTHWEST VIA ST. LOUIS AND CINCINNATI.

....	9.00 am	Lv... MINNEAPOLIS... Ar	6.35 pm	....
....	9.15 am	Lv........St. Paul........Ar	6.30 pm	....
....	6.00 pm	Lv......Des Moines......Ar	9.00 am	....
....	7.30 am	Ar.......St. Louis.......Lv	8.25 pm	....
....	4.10 pm	Lv........Omaha........Ar	12.45 n'n	....
....	8.35 pm	Lv.....Kansas City.....Ar	7.00 am	....
....	7.30 am	Ar.......St. Louis.......Lv	8.25 pm	....
....	8.00 am	Lv.......St. Louis.......Ar	6.25 pm	....
....	5.54 pm	Ar......Cincinnati......Lv	8.26 am	....
....	7.30 pm	Lv......Cincinnati......Ar	7.20 am	....
....	6.10 am	Ar....HARROGATE....Lv	9.25 pm	....

Sleeping cars through from St. Paul, Minneapolis, Omaha and Kansas City to St. Louis, St. Louis to Cincinna i and Cincinnati to Harrogate.

HOW TO REACH HARROGATE

(Cumberland Gap Park and Four Seasons Hotel)

FROM NORTH AND NORTHEAST VIA CINCINNATI.

....	6.30 pm	Lv.....NEW YORK.....Ar	8.00 am	....
....	9.20 pm	Lv.....Philadelphia.....Ar	5.25 am	....
....	7.00 am	Lv......Pittsburgh......Ar	7.15 pm	....
....	1.55 pm	Lv......Columbus......Ar	11.30 am	....
....	5.30 pm	Ar......Cincinnati......Lv	8.00 am	....
....	8.00 pm	Lv......New York......Ar	7.45 am	....
....	11.55 pm	Lv........Albany........Ar	3.45 am	....
....	6.55 am	Lv........Buffalo........Ar	7.20 pm	....
....	11.50 am	Lv......Cleveland......Ar	2.40 pm	....
....	7.10 pm	Ar......Cincinnati......Lv	7.30 am	....
....	7.55 am	Lv........Detroit........Ar	6.20 pm	....
....	10.15 am	Lv........Toledo........Ar	4.00 pm	....
....	5.05 pm	Ar......Cincinnati......Lv	9.00 am	....
....	7.30 pm	Lv......Cincinnati......Ar	7.20 am	....
....	6.10 am	Ar....HARROGATE....Lv	9.25 pm	....

Sleeping cars through from all above cities to Cincinnati, and Cincinnati to Harrogate.

FROM EAST AND NORTHEAST VIA NORTON.

....	5.00 pm	Lv.....NEW YORK.....Ar	4.00 pm	....
....	7.40 pm	Lv.....Philadelphia.....Ar	1.25 pm	....
....	10.25 pm	Lv......Harrisburg......Ar	10.25 am	....
....	9.54 pm	Lv......Baltimore......Ar	10.45 am	....
....	11.15 pm	Lv......Washington......Ar	9.30 am	....
....	11.45 pm	Lv........Norfolk........Ar	8.00 am	....
....	7.35 am	Lv......Lynchburg......Ar	1.10 am	....
....	9.25 am	Lv........Roanoke........Ar	11.15 pm	....
....	5.25 pm	Lv........Norton........Ar	1.35 pm	....
....	8.50 pm	Ar....HARROGATE....Lv	6.45 am	....

Sleeping cars through from all the above cities to Roanoke, and Roanoke to Harrogate.

FROM WEST AND SOUTHWEST VIA MEMPHIS.

10.35 pm	11.15 am	Lv......MEMPHIS......Ar	5.30 am	5.30 am
1.52 am	3.05 pm	Lv........Milan........Ar	1.52 am	1.52 am
8.50 am	10.35 pm	Lv... Bowling Green ...Ar	6.46 pm	6.46 pm
9.35 pm	10.00 am	Lv.... Lebanon Junc....Ar	4.17 pm	4.17 pm
6.10 am	7.20 pm	Ar....HARROGATE....Lv	9.25 pm	6.53 am

Sleeping cars through from Memphis to Lebanon Junction, and from thence to Harrogate without change.

Round Trip Tickets at Low Rates on Sale to Harrogate from principal cities of the country.

For any further information, for Rates, Sleeping Car Reservations, etc., call on or write to

SAM B. JONES, General Agent, - - - - - 381 Broadway, NEW YORK.
JNO. E. BURKE, Eastern Passenger Agent, - - 381 Broadway, NEW YORK.
HERMAN HOLMES, Traveling Passenger Agent, - - - - MEDINA, O.
C. L. SPRAGUE, Traveling Passenger Agent, - - - - DETROIT, MICH.
S. F. B. MORSE, Division Passenger Agent, - - - - CINCINNATI, O.
SID. J. GATES, Traveling Passenger Agent, - - - - - CINCINNATI, O.
W. H. HOYLAND, Passenger Agent, - - Fifth and Vine Sts., CINCINNATI, O.
J. A. CASSELL, Ticket Agent, - - - Fifth and Vine Sts., CINCINNATI, O.
W. S. McCHESNEY, Jr., General Agent, - - - - - LEXINGTON, KY.
W. H. HARRISON, Passenger Agent, - - - - - - LEXINGTON, KY.
GEO. L. CROSS, Northwestern Passenger Agent, 6 Rookery Building, CHICAGO, ILL.
C. C. W. ALFRIEND, Pass. Agent, S. W. Cor. Fourth and Main Sts., LOUISVILLE, KY.
J. H. MILLIKEN, Dist. Pass. Agent, S. W. Cor. Fourth and Main Sts., LOUISVILLE, KY.
J. A. STELTENKAMP, Traveling Passenger Agent, - - - LOUISVILLE, KY.
GEO. B. HORNER, Division Passenger Agent, 206 N. Broadway, ST. LOUIS, MO.
R. S. MARTIN, City Ticket Agent, - - - 206 N. Broadway, ST. LOUIS, MO.
W. E. ATMORE, City Passenger Agent, - - 206 N. Broadway, ST. LOUIS, MO.
C. H. FITZGERALD, Western Passenger Agent, - - - - KANSAS CITY, MO.
G. T. O'BRYAN, Ticket Agent, - - - - - - - - EVANSVILLE, IND.
JNO. A. SCOTT, District Passenger Agent, - - - - - MEMPHIS, TENN.
MAX BAUMGARTEN, City Ticket Agent, - - - - - - MEMPHIS, TENN.

Y. VAN DEN BERG, Traffic Manager. C. P. ATMORE, Gen'l Passenger Agent.

LOUISVILLE, KY.

This busy train schedule from the early 1890s illustrates the high hopes of Alexander Arthur and others who expected the developments around Cumberland Gap to lure visitors by the thousands. It also serves to show how connected the gap had become to places that were in their infancy when Boone and his followers first made the journey. (Courtesy of ALLM of LMU.)

In this photograph from the 1890s, the Louisville & Nashville Railroad (L&N) crosses the trestle near Fern Lake as it passes Middlesboro. The L&N completed its line from Pineville south to the gap in August 1889, joining up with the northbound Knoxville, Cumberland Gap & Louisville line that had made it to the gap just one week earlier. (Courtesy of BCHS.)

In this undated photograph taken from the Kentucky side of Cumberland Gap, the trestle of the railroad can be seen in the middle distance. Juxtaposed with that symbol of progress are horses and wagons traveling the old Wilderness Road, much as their forefathers did more than a century before. The wagon in the right foreground is roughly where the park visitor center stands today.

This mail wagon is shown on the Kentucky side of the gap. The Wilderness Road remained the primary route between the local communities in all three states, even after the advent of the railroad.

This undated photograph shows the Wilderness Road near the saddle of the gap. Telephone lines in the background indicate that this is the early 20th century but before 1907, when work began on the Object Lesson Road. The poor state of the road can clearly be seen here, with loose rocks and ruts making travel dangerous and leading to its reputation as "the Devil's Stairway."

When the railroad was completed under Cumberland Mountain, many assumed that the modern method of train travel had made roads obsolete. But use of the Wilderness Road in fact increased, as people still needed to transport goods locally and access the train stations. The increased use strained the old Wilderness Road more than ever.

When the Office of Public Roads of the US Department of Agriculture began to select road sections throughout the country for upgrades to varied types of paving, the tristate area banded together and requested that the neglected Wilderness Road through the gap be considered. Once funds were secured, work began on this Object Lesson Road in July 1907.

Macadam was first used in the United States in Maryland in 1822. Invented by John McAdam, the pavement was created by binding small, angular stones together with an aggregate, and then compacting the surface. Larger stones were crushed for use to conform to a uniform size, one smaller than tire width. Here, a roller was used to compact the surface rather than the traditional reliance on road traffic.

When completed, the two-mile Object Lesson Road delivered riders a smooth, graded road of no more than a nine-percent grade. The road opened to great celebration, and enthusiasm for the improvement led Kentucky state representative Joe Bosworth to lobby for a statewide road improvement program to "get Kentucky out of the mud."

Indian Rock, seen here in 1924, is one of the few remaining landmarks that were mentioned in early travel accounts. Reputed to be a spot favored by Native Americans from which to ambush settlers, it was later used for much the same purpose by highwaymen in the lawless post–Civil War days. Here, the legendary rock has been reduced to a billboard.

Two

Pre-park Communities

This was our playground.

—Betty Jo Goforth Pittman, former resident of Cumberland Gap

At just over 24,000 acres, Cumberland Gap National Historical Park is one of the largest National Park Service areas east of the Mississippi. Unlike many of the larger western national parks, however, the projected location of the park encompassed a number of long-standing small communities.

Families who lived in these communities could trace their ancestors back to the earliest days of westward settlement. Instead of passing through Cumberland Gap and continuing northwest, they elected to stay in the area. Some created family enclaves in the hollows of the mountains and some helped to establish small towns, like Middlesboro and Cumberland Gap. Wherever they settled, they built homes, worked the land, and created a life for their children and their children's children.

Much of the time between the authorization of the park in 1940 and the dedication in 1959 was spent acquiring this land. This process was relatively straightforward in Tennessee, which contained just 10 percent of the total acreage, and most in corporate ownership. But the portion of southwestern Virginia destined for the park was home to several families who were bitter about having to give up their traditional livelihoods of logging, mining, and hunting.

More than half of the land for the park lay in the economically disadvantaged Kentucky counties of Bell and Harlan. While the town of Middlesboro wholeheartedly supported the park, many small landowners were not enthusiastic about it and, like the families in Virginia, faced condemnation of their property in the courts.

Many of these former residents and their descendants were interviewed as part of the park's 50th anniversary commemoration. Their honest and sometimes painful recollections of both living in and leaving the parklands were recorded, and in this way, some of the lingering negative feelings were acknowledged, allowing reconciliation to begin.

Preston Beason was the patriarch of a family who owned land in Kentucky at the time of the park's authorization. Beason died in the 1930s, but he had several family members still living in homes along the Davis Branch. The Beasons' property ended up being condemned, partly due to the difficulty of tracking down all the family members involved in the transfer, a not uncommon problem in the numerous parcels of land in the mountains. Below, members of the Beason family pose in front of their home; foundations and rock walls are still visible today. Family members have been interviewed by the park, and some descendants now volunteer and work at the national park. (Both, courtesy of the Rhodes family.)

One-room schoolhouses were still being used in the area when the park was authorized in 1940. This school served the Dark Ridge community, including the Beason and nearby Wilson families. In this 1929 photograph, Cassie Beason is in the second row, second from left, and Carrie Beason is in the third row, second from the right. (Courtesy of the Rhodes family.)

Another Kentucky family affected by the park was that of Rollan A. Marsee, who moved to the area in 1880. Rollan worked in the coal mines and gathered oak bark to sell for making tannin to cure animal hides. Marsee's sons and their families settled nearby. Here, George Marsee's family gathers at his funeral in 1945 near the community chapel. Only the cemetery survives today. (Courtesy of Shelva N. Marsee.)

The George Goforth home was one of many houses located in Virginia that was acquired for Cumberland Gap National Historical Park. It was located at the intersection of the Tennessee Road and the old Wilderness Road trail, both of which are restored today as walking paths. This early 1940s image of the home also shows the outbuildings as well as a car to the far left. Below, the home can be seen just left of center in the photograph taken from the town of Cumberland Gap. Not too far from the Iron Furnace, the Goforth home was one of several along the Tennessee Road.

The steps that the Goforth family is sitting on here are still visible today along the Tennessee Road trail. Betty Jo Goforth Pittman, the girl shown with her mother and little sister in the photographs, still visits the park to hike and visit her old homesite. She was interviewed in 2011. "If mom was living she'd still be angry," she recalled, adding, "Well, as bad as I hated to give up my homeplace, now I'm thankful, because there'd be trailers all over this place . . . that would be a heartbreak." (Both, courtesy of Betty Jo Goforth Pittman.)

This view of the White Rocks, as seen from Ewing, Virginia, shows the rural nature of the Virginia side of the park. White Rocks is an important geological feature and has significant historical connotations: weary travelers knew that once they reached this landmark on their journey west, it was just 10 miles to the Cumberland Gap.

The Chadwell Gap Coal Company (CGCC) mining operation was one of many such small operations that now lies within the park. The mining landscape—including coke ovens, mines (now gated), and tramlines—all form part of the National Register–eligible CGCC Historic District. The closing of the mine by the park was hard on local families, many of whom moved north to Michigan for work.

The Bert Hensley family was one of several families who moved west from North Carolina to settle atop Brush Mountain at the beginning of the 20th century, echoing the actions of the pioneers of a century earlier. Here, Bert and his wife, Linda, pose for a formal portrait with their children, from left to right, Jackson, Park, Betsann, Finley, Morgan, and Grant. (Courtesy of Nancy Gibbons Taylor.)

Members of the Hensley and Gibbons families pose in the cemetery on Decoration Day. From left to right are (first row) General Gibbons, Tip Hensley, an unidentified girl, Delsie Hensley, with Orville Gibbons behind her, and Lorene Gibbons; (second row) Ray Gibbons, Jess Gibbons, Finley Hensley, Elijah Gibbons, and his wife, Louanna, and son.

One of the sad facts of life on the isolated mountaintop in the first decades of the 20th century was the loss of many babies and children due to disease. Mable Hensley was one of three children of Park Hensley to die on the mountain. The graveyard is now part of the historic district, and the stones are given a new coat of whitewash each year as part of the traditional Decoration Day activities.

A one-room schoolhouse served the purposes of the families at the settlement. Teachers came from off the mountain and boarded with residents. One teacher, Stella Callahan, ended up marrying Wallace Hensley and staying in the community. In this photograph from the 1920s, the children of Hensley pose for the camera.

Earl Palmer, the "Blue Ridge Mountains' Roaming Cameraman," took many photographs of the people at Hensley in the 1930s and 1940s. This unidentified man cooks his supper under Indian Rock shelter on Brush Mountain, just down the ridge from the settlement. Palmer spent time with his subjects, and his respect for the people of the southern Appalachians is evident in his portraits.

Sherman Hensley was the patriarch of the Hensley family and the last to leave the settlement in 1951. He wanted his family to escape the progress of the 20th century and live in a simpler way, growing their own food and only leaving the mountain for necessities they couldn't make themselves. Below is the Willie Gibbons farm in the 1950s, when the park was established. Gibbons was the community blacksmith, and his shop is one of the tour stops today. Although 500 acres were cleared at the time of settlement, today the Hensley Historic District encompasses just 100 acres of maintained land and buildings.

Thomas Jefferson Cupp, a cousin of the Hensley family, was known as a bootlegger and local character. Photographer Earl Palmer described him as a man "known for his virtuosity around Chadwell Gap. Without a peer with a double-bitted axe in his strong hands . . . rail splitter par-excellence, rough feathered Tom was also a man to be reckoned with, pistol-wise—and the best maker of apple brandy around the hill country. Tom tended to his own bizzness [*sic*], however, never doing quite as well as he expected to, and never giving a damn if he didn't." His house, a popular meeting place for the men of the area, has been updated and now serves as a backcountry cabin.

The identity of the family pictured here is not known, but they lived near Chadwell Gap in Virginia. This iconic photograph of a typical family of Depression-era Appalachia is one of Earl Palmer's more gripping portraits. "I try to portray a person in his best light," Palmer once said.

Alexander Arthur was a Scotsman who visited the Cumberland Gap area after learning of the findings of the Harvard Geological School. Inspired by the stark beauty of the area and moved by its romantic desolation following the Civil War, Arthur envisioned another Pittsburgh in the Cumberland Mountains and founded Middlesboro, Kentucky, in 1888.

In photographs dating from 1890, the impressive Cumberland Gap can be seen in the background as building progressed on Cumberland Avenue, a grand avenue of businesses and homes that is part of a National Register Historic District today. Attracting emigrants from England, Italy, Germany, Eastern Europe, Greece, and Lebanon, Arthur's "Magic City" was a center of culture in the mountains at the turn of the 20th century. Later, it would become known for its rowdy lifestyle, as coal miners from the hills mixed with small-town gangsters of the 1930s and 1940s. Today, Middlesboro is a small town of approximately 12,000 residents.

Alexander Arthur's new city of Middlesboro needed a water supply, which he created by damming the winding Yellow Creek. The resultant Fern Lake immediately became a very popular recreational destination for residents of the city. The artificial lake is three miles long with a capacity for 900 million gallons of water. This postcard captures the beauty of the falls below the dam.

Fern Lake immediately became a popular recreational destination for city residents, as seen here in this 1890s photograph of a boating party.

The Fern Lake Fishing Club is a social club that dates from the early days of the lake and is still in existence today. For a fee, members could fish from the lake and use the boathouse for social occasions. One resident remembers fishing with her father below the boathouse. Today, the national park owns the land around the lake, but as of 2013, the lake itself is still in private hands.

Bartlett Park was a popular recreational Middlesboro park, with a dance hall and enormous swimming pool created from the damming up of Yellow Creek. Closed for a time following a polio scare, the pool was in operation for most of the 1930s. Today, the creek has been restored to its natural contours and is part of a popular park picnic area.

Earl Palmer captured this iconic scene of a baptism in the waters of Fern Lake in the late 1930s. Palmer described the scene: "Wint Bolton, Pastor of Cumberland Avenue Baptist Church in the late 30's and early 40's baptizes some of his congregation in the spill off from Fern Lake, something you don't see in this day and time."

The waters of Yellow Creek and other streams in the mountains were reputed to be crystal clear and so were conducive to the brewing of beer. Consequently, one of the more successful industries in Middlesboro was the New South Brewery and Ice Company. This imposing structure once stood within what is now the national park.

William Wallbrecht Sr. was the first general manager of the brewery and was succeeded by his son William Jr. Born on the ship on its voyage from Germany, Wallbrecht Sr. was also on the board of Arthur's American Association, Ltd., and is buried with his wife in the Middlesboro Cemetery.

The offices of the New South Brewery and Ice Company stood beside the brewery itself. The company employed a number of local men but went out of business in 1919 after the county went dry, with its attempts to sell nonalcoholic drinks failing. The magnificent brewery building was torn down soon after closing its doors. (Courtesy of Stephen Earle.)

New South promoted its local connections with its popular Pinnacle Beer. The girl in the logo was said to be a local mountain girl, Alice Lamb. Lamb later succumbed to the temptations of the city and fell into prostitution, meeting her death in a sordid room above a bar. Note the Temperance Drink, No. 23 and Daisy brands of nonalcoholic beverages.

English investors visit the Sterling Coal Mine. The contrast between the gentry of Middlesboro and Harrogate and the workers who made much of their lifestyle possible was obvious, and the area's struggles with unionization and inequities between owners and workers would become the stuff of legend, especially in Harlan County, Kentucky. (Courtesy of Clyde Mayes.)

Coal mining began in the Cumberland Gap area long before the development of the 1890s but wasn't an organized endeavor until the railroads linked Middlesboro with the rest of the country. No major coal companies were located in the lands that became the park, but several small mines had to close. Although difficult at the time, residents have expressed relief that the mountain scenery has been spared from the ravages of mining.

Coal wasn't the only valuable commodity to be had from the lands around Cumberland Gap. Since the time of earliest settlement, the lush Appalachian forests of poplar, chestnut, and oak had supplied residents with fuel for their homes and for their livelihoods. This Earl Palmer photograph shows a sawmill located near Middlesboro.

The town of Cumberland Gap grew as a result of the boom in railroad construction in the late 1880s. Workers lived in temporary houses and tents erected in the valley and soon, support businesses in the form of stores and saloons followed. This depot served the town for decades before the train no longer stopped in this small town.

This view, captured in the 1930s from the Pinnacle, shows Fern Lake in the top left background and Middlesboro at the right. Alexander Arthur's dreams for an industrial metropolis in the Appalachians were short-lived; fires and bank failures plagued him and his city for some time to come.

The rural nature of the Tennessee side of the gap is shown in this 1964 photograph. The Pinnacle can be seen on the right, rising more than 2,400 feet above sea level. Beyond the small towns of Cumberland Gap and Harrogate, the land is home to small farms and pockets of houses. The growth of Lincoln Memorial University, located in Harrogate and adjacent to the national park, has attracted more families to the area.

This view of the gap from the Little Tunnel Inn on US Highway 58 has not changed appreciably since the photograph was taken in the 1950s. The railroad here has become part of a trail system that winds in and out of the park and joins up with a longer greenway system in both Tennessee and Virginia. The inn, however, was closed in the 1980s, as construction for the highway tunnel made it inaccessible.

Lincoln Memorial University was chartered in 1897 and built on the site of the failed Four Seasons Hotel. Inspired by Pres. Abraham Lincoln's desire to reward the loyal citizens of east Tennessee during the Civil War, Union general O.O. Howard worked with Reverend A.A. Myers to establish a school for the mountain people. Today, the university is thriving and has opened a successful medical school. (Courtesy of ALLM of LMU.)

Three

The Growth of Tourism

The door left open by nature.

—*The Lure of Kentucky: A Historical Guide Book*, 1939

Although the importance of the Cumberland Gap as a navigable route through the mountains lessened as roads and tunnels were built along the Appalachians, interest in its scenic beauty increased. With the advent of the automobile and the creation of the paved Object Lesson Road over the mountain, driving through the gap became a goal in itself.

An ambitious road was built from the gap to the top of Cumberland Mountain (the Pinnacle), allowing the more courageous sightseers the opportunity to take in the sights atop the highest peak in the tristate area (for a slight fee, of course). In some places, the road followed the old military road laid down by Civil War troops of 60 years previous, and parts of that road can still be seen today in the park.

Another popular local attraction gained a national following when guided tours began in part of the Gap Cave system noted by early land speculator Dr. Thomas Walker in 1750. Commercial tours of the cave began in 1890, and it was soon renamed Cudjo's Cave as a tourism twist, playing on the popularity of J.T. Trowbridge's 1864 book of the same name.

A renewed interest and pride in America's history at this time inspired the National Society of the Daughters of the Revolution (DAR) to spearhead a charge to publicly commemorate Daniel Boone, whose importance in the country's growth had been largely forgotten in the rapid progress of the early 20th century. To this end, monuments marking Boone's Trail were erected in North Carolina, Virginia, Tennessee, and Kentucky. In a nod to the importance of Cumberland Gap as part of Boone's story, a monument linking all four states was placed in the saddle and unveiled in a grand celebration in June 1915.

Supporting businesses sprang up as these tourist attractions grew in popularity. Motels and tourist courts were built capitalizing on the country's love affair with their cars, and souvenir stands and restaurants weren't far behind.

The imposing nature of the Pinnacle on Cumberland Mountain made it tempting as an early destination for residents and visitors. The view encompasses all three states of Kentucky, Tennessee, and Virginia, as well as the Cumberland Gap itself. Here, an unidentified group perches on the rock overlooking the town of Cumberland Gap near where the overlook is today. Below, a group of Lincoln Memorial University students picnic at the top. Since there were no passable roads up the Pinnacle at the time these photographs were taken, these intrepid sightseers would have had to walk and sometimes climb up the rocky mountain. (Above, courtesy of Steve Moore; below, courtesy of ALLM of LMU.)

PLAN OF DEVELOPMENT

The American Association, Limited, will lease on Royalties its Coal, Iron, Clay, Timber, and Quarry privileges. It will rent cleared farms on reasonable terms. It will sell or lease lands suitable for manufacturing industries of all kinds.

MAPS, PLATS, FORMS OF LEASE, AND PARTICULARS AS TO

ROYALTIES, RENTS, AND PRICES,

FURNISHED ON APPLICATION TO

ALEXANDER A. ARTHUR, GENERAL MANAGER, KNOXVILLE, TENN.,

AND

E. E. MALCOLM, ASSISTANT MANAGER, MIDDLESBOROUGH, KY.

The Middlesborough Town Company

PROPOSES TO SELL BY AUCTION, **OCTOBER 14 TILL 19**

About 500 acres of Business, Residence and Villa Lots

TERMS OF SALE:

ONE-FOURTH CASH, BALANCE IN 1, 2, AND 3 YEARS, WITH SIX PER CENT. INTEREST.

Additional Sales—May, 1890, and October, 1890.

SPECIAL INDUCEMENTS OFFERED TO MANUFACTURERS AND INDUSTRIAL PLANTS.

TOWN PLATS, ETC., MAY BE HAD ON APPLICATION TO

ALEXANDER A. ARTHUR, GENERAL MANAGER, KNOXVILLE, TENN.,

AND

J. M. BROOKS, SALES AGENT, MIDDLESBOROUGH, KY.

The Cumberland Gap Park Company

Intends to erect and complete, in 1890, a HOTEL, SANITARIUM and CASINO, modelled after the celebrated Baths, etc., of Schwalbach, Homburg, Baden-Baden, Vichy, etc.

Alexander Arthur recognized the tourist potential immediately upon seeing the beauty of the Cumberland Gap area. This advertisement offers lots for both businesses and residences and makes mention of the Cumberland Gap Park Company, the driving force behind the construction of the Four Seasons complex. Another promotional publication extolling the virtues of Harrogate, Tennessee, boasts, "The location could not have been better selected for the building of a popular and fashionable resort which would attract tourists, pleasure-seekers and invalids from all parts of the world. In fact, it is the plan and intention of the directors to make Harrogate and Cumberland Gap Park the most attractive and picturesque summer and winter resorts in North America."

The Daughters of the American Revolution worked to locate and mark Daniels Boone's Trail through the states of North Carolina, Tennessee, Virginia, and Kentucky. In 1915, they placed a monument in the saddle of the Cumberland Gap that commemorated all four states and their roles in Boone's accomplishment. In the above photograph, the monument serves as a backdrop for the opening of the Skyland Road up the mountain. Governors Flemon D. Sampson of Kentucky and Myers Cooper of Ohio were just two of the dignitaries present. At left, World War I hero and Tennessee native Sgt. Alvin York lays a wreath on the monument during LMU's Pioneer's Day activities in June 1925. (Left, courtesy of ALLM of LMU.)

For reasons unclear today, the Bell Telephone Company installed a telephone beside the DAR Boone monument when it was unveiled, and the pole can be seen in this undated photograph. Note also the white arrows painted on the rocks and tree, presumably pointing to the monument.

This 1924 postcard shows a car on the highway as it approaches the Daniel Boone monument in the gap. Five years later, the monument was relocated 100 feet to make room for the construction of the Skyland Road up the mountain.

The opening of the Skyland Road up the Pinnacle was a grand occasion. Aside from an exciting attempt by LMU student Jess T. Rockwell to drive his Model T Ford up it in 1922, the Pinnacle had been accessible by foot only. Recognizing the tourism potential, Middlesboro businessman J.L Manring bought the mountain in 1928. He then formed the Skyland Company, and in just over a year, the road up the mountain was built.

Skyland Highway Opening June 4th 1929. Gov. Sampson of Kentucky and Gov. Cooper of Ohio Front Row Center.

The twisting nature of the new Skyland Road up to the Pinnacle allowed for interesting views into the Cumberland Gap and incorporated some hairpin turns, features which remain today. Unfortunately, the new road also cut across Civil War features, including forts and road traces.

This early aerial photograph illustrates the winding nature of the Skyland Road. The crushed-stone surface of the road made for a bit of a rough ride, but it certainly beat a two-mile hike. A small parking area and turnaround were paved at the summit.

In this undated photograph, two boys stand by a car parked near the same stone marker seen on page 25. Note the changes in road surface, vegetation, and grade between the two photographs, which were probably taken only 25 years apart.

With the Skyland Road making access to the Pinnacle much easier, the area around the junction of the road and the highway bisecting the gap began attracting commercial ventures, including a toll business. This photograph, dated Labor Day 1939, shows the sign with rates to the summit: 40¢ per person and 40¢ per car.

When visitors to the Pinnacle reached the top, they had to climb over rocks to reach the wooden platform overlooking the view into the gap and the three states. The wooden stand shown in this photograph replaced an earlier, smaller platform. The promotional brochure for the Pinnacle assured the visitor that the view from the top was "worth many times the amount charged."

This image of the saddle of Cumberland Gap in the 1930s shows a service station and car with a trailer parked behind it. The flat area in the center right marks the location of the Civil War earthwork of Fort McClellan, partially destroyed by the widening of the highway through the gap. Note the DAR marker on the far right.

In this 1942 photograph, the Edwards children pose at the saddle of the gap in front of painted rocks indicating the tristate meeting point. From left to right are Danny Lee Edwards holding Sharon, with Lloyd Francis and William Blaine standing in front. The Edwards family was traveling through on their way to live in Pennington Gap, Virginia. (Courtesy of Sharon Edwards Anderson.)

Also located in the saddle of the Gap was a display building containing a wooden loom. Described as being 113 years old, the loom was reputed to have connections with the Lincoln family. A state boundary sign marking the line between Kentucky and Virginia stands nearby, as does a Coca-Cola billboard urging passing motorists to "Visit the Pinnacle."

Another photograph taken on the Labor Day holiday in 1939 shows a souvenir stand and information center, letting visitors know that they were indeed standing in the Cumberland Gap. Drinks, candy, postcards, and ice cream were sold there.

These two Kentucky state historical markers were placed on the highway through the Cumberland Gap in 1929. The front sign gives a brief history of the significance of the gap, while the second relates the history of Kentucky's admittance to the Union in 1792.

The service station and replication blockhouse can be seen here, along with a sign pointing across the highway to the Skyland Road entrance. The 1915 DAR Boone monument can be seen just to the upper left behind the blockhouse, where it was moved during construction of the road up the Pinnacle.

Even before Dr. Thomas Walker made note of Gap Cave in 1750, animals and Native Americans had made use of the extensive caverns located along the Wilderness Road. In 1890, G.B. Cockrell opened it for tours and called it King Solomon's Cave. Some years later, the name was changed to Cudjo's Cave to capitalize on the popularity of J.T. Trowbridge's 1864 book of the same name. The postcard above shows the ticket booth and store on the left, with the cave entrance on the right. Some residents recall that the dash across the highway was the most exciting part of the cave tour. At right, students from LMU visit the cave in their Sunday best. The electrical lights and handrails were removed during the park's restoration of the area in the 1990s, and today, tours are conducted by flashlight. (Right, courtesy of ALLM of LMU.)

All the tourists visiting the Cumberland Gap needed places to stay and several inns and motels opened to fulfill that need. Above, the Indian Rock Inn and Café (Indian Rock is just to the right of the parking lot) had the reputation of being more of a bar than a restaurant. Betty Jo Goforth remembers hearing drunken men walking past her house on the Tennessee Road on their way home after a night at the inn. Below, the Little Tunnel Inn grew from a small log structure to a modern motel and restaurant. The Little Tunnel Inn was also known as the last place to buy alcohol before crossing into Kentucky from Tennessee.

Harris Courts was located at the base of the mountain on the Kentucky side of the gap, as seen in this postcard. Below, the Cumberland Mountain Hotel and Cottages also had a restaurant and gift shop. Middlesboro resident Freda Van Bever, who worked there in the early 1950s, remembers the good reputation of the restaurant's Sunday dinners and the friendly working atmosphere. Walter Gibbons, a resident of the Hensley Settlement, helped to build the attractive stone buildings, remnants of which can still be seen in the park today.

This promotional brochure typified the national love affair with the automobile in the 1930s as promoters sought to sell domestic travel. Published by the Cumberland Association of cities in the tristate area, the brochure boasted that, "The Cumberland People are famous for their hospitality." Liberties were taken with the illustrations; the landscape resembles the Rocky Mountains more than the Appalachians.

Four

The Coming of the National Park

This is a wonderful thing, this park.

—Vice Pres. Richard M. Nixon, park dedication speech, July 3, 1959

The first mention of establishing a national park at Cumberland Gap was made during a session of the Appalachian Logging Conference in 1922. But the act creating the park would not be signed into law for 18 years. Why such a delay?

There was no doubt in many people's minds that Cumberland Gap was worthy of national park status. Its unique natural features coupled with its importance in the history of westward migration of the country made it a perfect candidate for preservation on a national scale. But its significance was not easy to pinpoint. Unlike the other national parks of the day, it didn't just commemorate a battle, a landmark, or a person. Cumberland Gap played a role in the history of Native Americans, pioneers, the Civil War, and industrialization. Its natural features included caves, peaks, wildlife, and waterfalls.

Consequently, most of those 18 years were spent finding the words that accurately conveyed why the Cumberland Gap deserved to be protected. Kentucky congressman John M. Robsion spent years trying to formulate a successful theme for the proposed park; ideas included a Lincoln Park with a carving on the Pinnacle and a Civil War park with statues of Grant and Lee in the saddle. Others felt the gap should be more of a recreational area for use rather than conservation.

Finally, in June 1940, House of Representatives Bill 9394 authorizing the park was signed into law by Pres. Franklin D. Roosevelt, reading, in part, "that such area or areas shall include, at least, the following features and intervening lands: Cumberland Gap, the Pinnacle, the remaining fortifications of the War Between the States, Soldiers Cave, King Solomon's Cave, etc." Unique to this day in national parks, Cumberland Gap could not be distilled into one period or element of significance.

But the hardest work was yet to come—that of acquiring the land, hiring staff, and building the infrastructure. Another 19 years would pass before the new Cumberland Gap National Historical Park was formally dedicated during a memorably hot weekend in July 1959.

Cumberland Gap Should Be Preserved as National Park!

● America has developed a great national park system, but the work has not been completed. Many scenic and historic assets remain unprotected and undeveloped.

● Cumberland Gap in the center of the scenic region where Kentucky, Tennessee, and Virginia join is one of these neglected spots. It should be a national park!

● We believe that now is the logical time to present this proposition to the National Park Service in Washington, in order to secure their recommendation that this great historic shrine may be brought under the control of the federal government.

● We do not know of another locality in the United States which should so commend itself as a national park possibility. As the pioneer gateway to the North and West, made sacred by the footprints of Dr. Thomas Walker, the first white man to enter the Dark and Bloody Ground of the Wilderness of Kentucky, and Daniel Boone, the trail blazer for the new Western empire, this historic pass stands pre-eminent in American traditions of greatness.

● Through Cumberland Gap the Indians passed back and forth on their hunting expeditions. The buffaloes which roamed the wilderness followed along the broken trails through the forest. With the coming of the white man, it became a beaten path, first for the lone hunters, then for the settlers, and later for the traders. Through Cumberland Gap an empire was established, and a nation grew to young manhood.

● When our country was plunged into Civil War, it was Cumberland Gap that became a strategic outpost, over which the Federal and Confederate armies struggled for possession. Huge trenches and breastworks still wind around the mountainside, unmarked, forgotten, and all but obliterated.

● The great Henry Clay, in one of his campaigns, rode into the heart of the Cumberlands, and stopped on a hilltop somewhere in this vicinity. He listened to the silent voices of the forest. His companion wanted to know what he was doing. Said Mr. Clay:

● "I am listening to the coming millions!"

● The millions have come. Humanity has followed back and forth in the ebb and flood tide of commerce. Highways have converged at this union of three great Southern states, and Cumberland Gap still remains a gateway for the nation.

● Silent and brooding, the giant Pinnacle looks down upon the pass and the valleys below, a Midland Gibralter of America. From Pinnacle Crest seven states can be viewed in the distance. No more superb view can be found anywhere in the nation.

● Truly the spot is hallowed ground. For miles and miles in every direction, the mountain peaks nestle close and beautiful. Most of this mountain land is in timber, and most of it should be conserved for the future. The national government should take a hand, and hold this wide sweep of the Cumberlands pristine in its glory for America's posterity.

● The Pine Mountain State Park, touching the bend of the majestic Cumberland River as it hurries down out of the Harlan coal fields, should be an added nucleus for this national park. Here the first camp site of white settlers is preserved. Mountain streams, pure and clear, feed into the river from the Clear Creek Mountain Springs section, also an ideal integral portion of the proposed park.

● It would be easy to provide the necessary acreage of forest land contiguous to the Cumberland Gap section for a national park. We feel sure that if the proposition were presented properly to the officials of the Department of Interior it would be received with sympathy and favor. A Cumberland Gap National Park would be an important link in the National Park system of the South.

The August 10, 1935, edition of the *Middlesboro Daily News* ran this editorial calling for the establishment of the park. Accompanied by photographs of the various attractions of the gap, the piece also called for the Pine Mountain State Park in Kentucky, 14 miles away, to be included, a possibility under consideration at one time. The writer also predicted that it "would be easy" to provide the necessary acreage for the park.

Kentucky congressman John M. Robsion was a tireless advocate for the creation of a national park at Cumberland Gap. His efforts to create a bill that would pass both houses included attempts to frame the park as Lincoln National Park and as a Civil War memorial complete with markers and tablets similar to Gettysburg.

$______ No.______

Certificate of Membership

Cumberland Gap National Historical Park Association

Incorporated

This Certifies That

______

HAS SUBSCRIBED ______ MEMBERSHIP

IN THE CUMBERLAND GAP NATIONAL HISTORICAL PARK ASSOCIATION, FOR THE PRESERVATION OF THE NATURAL BEAUTY AND EVIDENCES OF HISTORICAL SIGNIFICANCE OF THE CUMBERLAND GAP AREA OF TENNESSEE, KENTUCKY AND VIRGINIA, AND THE ESTABLISHMENT IN THE AREA OF A NATIONAL HISTORICAL PARK AND RECREATIONAL CENTER.

IN WITNESS WHEREOF WE HAVE SUBSCRIBED OUR NAMES AND AFFIXED THE SEAL OF THE CORPORATION AT MIDDLESBORO, KENTUCKY, THIS ______ DAY OF ______.

______ PRESIDENT

______ SECRETARY-TREASURER

CUMBERLAND GAP NATIONAL HISTORICAL PARK ASSOCIATION INC. 1938

To help build support and raise funds for the hoped-for national park, the Cumberland Gap National Historical Park Association (CGNHPA) was created in 1938 after the National Park Service surveyed the gap for its possible inclusion into the park system. Membership in the organization was offered at three levels: $2 annual, $25 sustaining, and $100 founders.

On August 28, 1943, Kentucky governor Keen Johnson, Virginia governor Colgate W. Darden Jr., and Tennessee governor Prentice Cooper (pictured left to right) met at the tristate marker to formally agree to procure lands from their respective states for the creation of the national park. Direct purchase by the federal government was prohibited in the park's enabling legislation.

Lands to be included in the new national park included both scenic and historical treasures. This photograph by Earl Palmer of a man on Chimney Rock captures the awe-inspiring nature of the surrounding countryside. Palmer's original caption describes the view as "the miracle of God's handiwork . . . the bathing of ancient and neighboring cliffs with sun-splashed silver."

Although the construction of US Highway 25E obliterated the ancient Wilderness Road through the gap itself, portions of the road remained in many places when the park was established. Here is one of the sections as it appeared in 1956, looking much like it must have back in Daniel Boone's time.

Park employees Jess Stamey and Virginia Huff pose atop the White Rocks in Lee County, Virginia, in 1962. These 400-foot cliffs allow intrepid hikers a panoramic view of the Virginia countryside and are home to a rare lichen and a pair of peregrine falcons. Huff recalled in an oral interview many decades later that getting out in the park was one of her favorite parts of her job as superintendent's assistant.

When Sherman Hensley left Hensley Settlement in 1951, it didn't take long for nature to reclaim the wooden buildings. Willie Gibbons's barn, shown here in the mid-1950s, succumbed to the fate of many old buildings when left unmaintained. Restoring the settlement was (and remains) a full-time job at the park.

The Pinnacle had drawn visitors for decades before it became a part of the park. In 1955, the park built a parking lot, shelter, and restrooms to accommodate the growing number of visitors. While working, park employees found evidence of occupation by Civil War forces, and the bullets and grapeshot uncovered during that early construction helped form the basis of the park's museum collection.

Another one of the improvements at the Pinnacle included the construction of a larger and more secure viewing platform to replace the decades-old wooden stairs. The new overlook used native stone and allowed many more visitors access to the stunning view of three states. The shape was a heart, to symbolize Cumberland Gap as the heart of the Cumberlands.

For many years, this was the view from the Pinnacle Overlook. Directly below lies the small town of Cumberland Gap, Tennessee, with its street grid and adjoining hamlet of Tiprell. In the upper left of the photograph, the highway snakes past Lincoln Memorial University, while the lower left road continues into Virginia. Kentucky lies to the right, just out of the frame of the photograph.

The view from the Pinnacle Overlook has always been one of the most popular sights in the park and one of the easiest points to access in a hurry. In this image from the late 1950s, visitors can be seen walking up the path back to the parking lot after taking in the view.

The first ceremony held at the new park was the dedication of the new interpretive shelter built at the Pinnacle. On September 1, 1957, a ribbon cutting was held at the parking lot and the day was declared Establishment Day, marking the official opening of the park to the public. Robert Kincaid, then LMU president and staunch advocate of the park, addressed the crowd. Kincaid had been instrumental in the creation of the park from its earliest days, serving as president of the CGNHPA and writing editorials in the newspaper.

The interpretive shelter at the Pinnacle featured exhibits on the various periods of history encompassed at the park. Here, members of the National Lincoln Civil War Council visit the Pinnacle in 1958. From left to right are Holman Hamilton, Carl Maverly, William Townsend, and Ralph Newman.

In 1958, the park released information cards promoting various attractions. This card explained the geology that made the physical anomaly of the Cumberland Gap possible, but also provides an excellent view of the new Pinnacle Overlook and the rugged terrain of the Cumberland Mountain range. The Cumberland Gap itself is in the bottom right of the photograph.

Superintendent's assistant Virginia Huff and historian Hobart Cawood pose by the park sign at the first headquarters of the park in 1955. Located in just one room of the Hotel Cumberland in Middlesboro, Kentucky, the office held four employees.

In the early days of the park, the ranger's job was to explore as much of the 20,000 acres as he could. Today, some of the place names and locations have faded away, as in the case of Sheer Rock Lodge, north of Rhinoceros Rock. The ranger and his companion appear to be taking notes.

Big Saltpeter Cave, seen in this early 1960s photograph, contained remains of wooden troughs used to collect the leach brine from the hoppers in the process of saltpeter production for gunpowder. It is believed that these artifacts date from before the Civil War. Historian A.M. Loveless documented many of the extant conditions of the park at the time of establishment. The identity of this park employee is unknown.

Research into the park's many historical resources was a priority in the early days of development. Several archeological investigations were conducted, including one at the site of the early-19th-century iron furnace. An excavation behind the standing iron furnace was conducted in 1957 by NPS archeologist Jackson Moore. Such excavations allow the park to better relate the history of the sites within their care to the public.

Not every visitor to national parks is interested in scenery or culture. A law enforcement division is crucial to the smooth operation of a park. Here, a working still was found within the park by early rangers. Although a staple of the local culture for years, this and other traditional occupations such as ginseng hunting are illegal under the park regulations.

In February 1959, a contingent of Middlesboro residents traveled to Washington, DC, to invite Pres. Dwight D. Eisenhower to speak at the dedication of the park. Eisenhower accepted, but the death of his secretary of state later caused him to cancel. Among the congressmen pictured are Congressman Eugene Siler of Kentucky, Sen. Thruston Morton of Kentucky, Congressman Harry Fugate of Virginia, Sen. Estes Kefauver of Tennessee, Sen. Harry Byrd of Virginia, Sen. John Sherman Cooper of Kentucky, and Congressman Carroll Reece of Tennessee. Also included are several Middlesboro citizens, including Harry Hoe, Lawrence Russell, Maurice Henry, Clinton Broadwater, and Lee Campbell. (Courtesy of the Dwight D. Eisenhower Presidential Library & Museum.)

President Eisenhower sent his vice president, Richard M. Nixon, to the dedication instead after being urged to honor his commitment to the park dedication committee. Nixon flew to Middlesboro on July 3 and stayed several hours. One of the highlights of the dedication weekend was the parade down Cumberland Avenue. Here, Nixon waves to the crowd, estimated to number more than 20,000 people.

Remembered by many residents as the biggest day in Middlesboro's history, the parade was the product of months of planning by parade chairman Marvin Mayhall. In an oral interview, Mayhall recalled the hectic pace of the day. Floats representing every phase of the area's history, as well as the traditional beauty queens, celebrated the arrival of the park.

Vice President Nixon stopped at the Hotel Cumberland to view the rest of the parade and hobnob with other dignitaries. Nixon fully endorsed the new park, proclaiming that, "Cumberland Gap National Historical Park will provide new inspiration to keep alive the pioneer spirit that is the strength of America." From left to right are Kentucky senators John S. Cooper and Thruston B. Morton, Nixon, and Virginia senator Absalom W. Robertson.

Cumberland Gap National Historical Park superintendent Millard "Dean" Guy was on hand at the Pinnacle to welcome Nixon as he toured the park. While admiring the view from the overlook, Nixon observed that it was quite possible his ancestors had traveled through the Cumberland Gap from Pennsylvania.

Middlesboro police chief Ernest Mike was assigned the job of driving Nixon around town and the park during his visit and took his responsibility seriously. During an oral history interview with Mike many years later, he recalled his instructions from the FBI to not let anyone near the car. Mike can be seen here on the right, keeping an eye on the brand new Cadillac purchased for the occasion.

Vice Pres. Richard M. Nixon signs the guest book at the Pinnacle interpretive shelter while an unidentified boy watches intently. Nixon enjoyed his visit to the park, observing that, "This is a wonderful thing, this park. We must not allow our civilization as it advances to destroy all our natural beauty."

After the parade and visit from Nixon on July 3, the Fourth of July dawned hot for the serious business of dedicating the park. Arriving at the Middlesboro airport that day are, from left to right, R.M. Watt, chairman of the Kentucky National Parks Commission; Robert L. Kincaid, president of the CGNHPA; Fred A. Seaton, the Secretary of the Interior; Howard Douglass, secretary of the Kentucky National Park Commission; and Conrad Wirth, director of the National Park Service.

Howard Douglass (second from the left) and Kentucky senator Thruston Morton (far right) can be seen here with Middlesboro resident and chairman of the park dedication committee Harry Hoe (third from the left). Hoe, a decorated World War II veteran and prominent local citizen, was a driving force behind the arrangements for the dedication.

Secretary of the Interior Fred Seaton (left) and NPS director Conrad Wirth ham it up while touring the brand-new visitor center for the park. In his remarks at the dedication, Seaton noted that, "This is a place hallowed by history. . . . The history of an expanding, restless people, exploring whatever was ahead, crossing old boundaries, breaking rails, and building new roads through the wilderness . . . pushing ever on westward."

Cumberland Gap National Historical Park

MIDDLESBORO, KENTUCKY

DEDICATION EVENTS

FRIDAY, JULY 3

8:30 A.M.	Official Opening Park Visitor Center
9:00 A.M.	Historic Window Displays - Middlesboro Business District;
10:00 A.M.	Visitation of Points of Interest: Park Exhibit Rooms, Skyland Road and Pinnacle, Cudjo's Cave, Oldest American Golf Course - Middlesboro Country Club, Lincoln Room - Lincoln Memorial University.
	Golf Match and Exhibition - Middlesboro Country Club.
12:00 Noon	Parade - Cumberland Avenue (30th Street to 12th.) Hon. Richard M. Nixon, Vice President of the United States, reviewing.
2:30 P.M.	Aerial Salute - Air Force F-100 Jet Bombers Fourth Tactical Fighter Wing, Seymour Johnson Air Force Base.
3:00 P.M.	Band Concert - Cumberland Hotel Plaza
	Band Concert - Fountain Square
5:00 P.M.	Homecoming Supper (Boxes available at convenient points)
7:30 P.M.	Homecoming Jamboree - Bradner Stadium; Square Dancing - West Cumberland Avenue; Dancing - Junior High School Gym; Rock-N-Roll - Joyland Skating Rink; Dancing - Middlesboro Country Club.

SATURDAY, JULY 4

9:00 A.M.	Pinnacle Tours
12:00 Noon	Nations first Parade of the 49 State Flags - Cumberland Avenue to Visitor Center
	Official Luncheon - Middlesboro Country Club (Invitation)
2:00 P.M.	Dedication of Cumberland Gap National Historical Park - Visitor Center

Musical Overture............*101st Airborne Division Band*
WARRANT OFFICER EUGENE W. ALLEN, BAND MASTER

Presiding......................................*Conrad L. Wirth*
DIRECTOR, NATIONAL PARK SERVICE

The National Anthem......*101st Airborne Division Band*

Invocation....................................*Dr. W. F. Pettus*
DISTRICT SUPERINTENCENT, METHODIST CHURCH

Greetings......................................*Millard D. Guy*
SUPERINTENDENT, CUMBERLAND GAP
NATIONAL HISTORICAL PARK

Introductions..*Elbert Cox*
REGIONAL DIRECTOR, REGION ONE
NATIONAL PARK SERVICE

America the Beautiful......................*Miss Louisa Hoe*
DIRECTOR OF MUSIC
LINCOLN MEMORIAL UNIVERSITY

Introduction of Speaker......................*Conrad L. Wirth*

Dedication Address.......*The Honorable Fred A. Seaton*
SECRETARY OF THE INTERIOR

Stars & Stripes Forever...*101st Airborne Division Band*

Benediction......................*Rev. Father Otto M. Hering*
PASTOR, ST. JULIAN CATHOLIC CHURCH

4:00 P.M.	Official Reception (Invitation)
10:00 P.M.	Fireworks Display - Bradner Stadium

CUMBERLAND GAP — *Pathway of the Pioneers*

WHERE KENTUCKY, TENNESSEE, AND VIRGINIA MEET

COOPERATING AGENCIES

National Park Service - Department of Interior - United States of America

Dedication Committee - Cumberland Gap National Historical Park - Middlesboro, Kentucky

A glance through this official brochure of the dedication of Cumberland Gap National Historical Park shows the variety of activities planned for the weekend of July 3 and 4 in 1959. Besides the parade and speeches, the city of Middlesboro hosted a golf match, band concerts, historical window displays in their downtown business district, and evening dances. Tours of the Pinnacle, Cudjo's Cave, and the Skyland Road were offered by park staff. Fireworks concluded the festive weekend.

The stand for the dedication speeches was set up on the lawn of the new visitor center. The 101st Airborne Division Band played several rousing patriotic airs. Superintendent's assistant Virginia Huff and others who attended that day remember it as being one of the hottest of the summer, a fact borne out by the umbrellas used by some as shade.

The Nation's First Parade of the 49 State Flags was performed by the local Boy Scout troop. Alaska had just become a state, and the parade at the park dedication was the first time its flag was displayed. The flags were then placed along the walkway to the visitor center. They were donated to the park by the city of Middlesboro and are still flown on special occasions.

Cumberland Gap NHP superintendent Dean Guy addresses the crowd at the dedication while (from left to right) Senator Morton, Secretary of the Interior Seaton, and NPS director Wirth listen. Morton was a descendant of Dr. Thomas Walker, a land surveyor credited with being the first white man to travel through the Cumberland Gap. Much of what is known about the early history of the area is attributed to Walker's journal.

National Park Service regional director Elbert Cox prepares to cut the ribbon, marking the official opening of the new visitor center at the park, aided by Jan and Ann Guy, daughters of park superintendent Dean Guy.

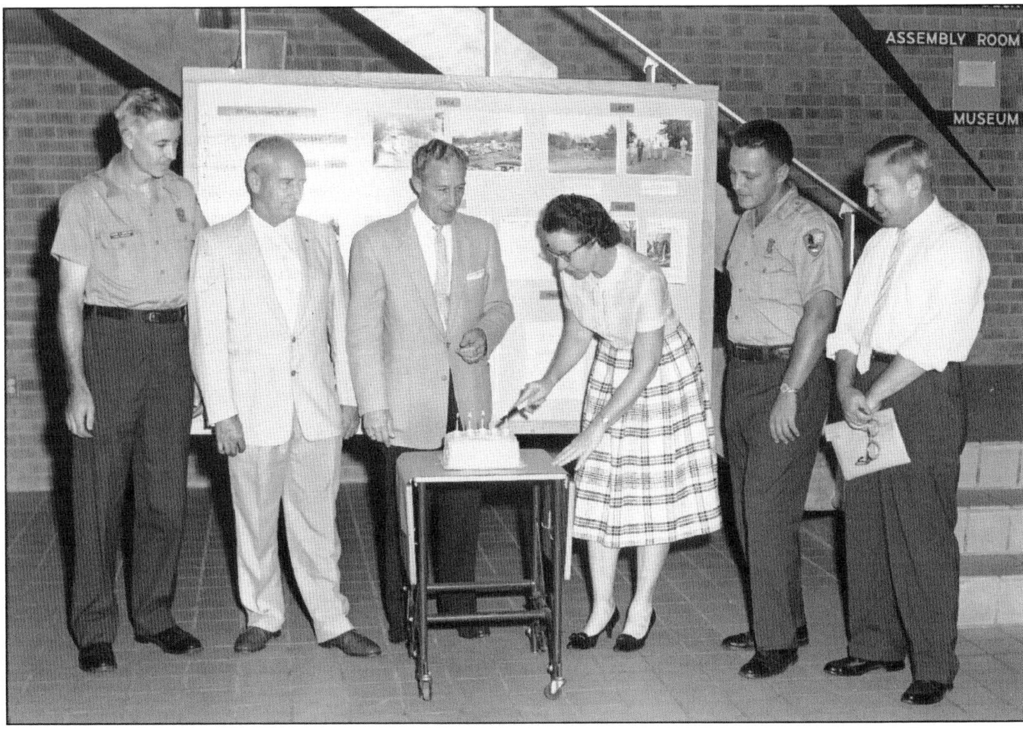

The park had its share of celebrations during its first few years. Here, the fifth anniversary of Establishment Day is celebrated with a cake. Chief ranger Lloyd Abelson (far left) and Virginia Huff stand in front of an exhibit about the Pinnacle facilities.

The visitor center was part of the Mission 66 initiative, a 10-year program to improve upon the infrastructure of the national parks in time for the 50th birthday of the National Park Service in 1966. NPS director Conrad Wirth proposed the program, which resulted in a number of modern streamlined visitor centers in parks, including the one at Cumberland Gap.

The new visitor center contained a museum for visitors to learn more about the history and natural features of the park. Exhibits illustrated the history of the many eras represented at Cumberland Gap, from Native Americans to pioneers to the Civil War and industrialization. Due to the newness of the park, most of the exhibits contained items on loans from other parks and the Smithsonian Institution that didn't always accurately portray the gap's history. When the visitor center was remodeled as part of the restoration efforts of the early 2000s, artifacts originating from Cumberland Gap were included and text was updated to reflect an increased understanding of the area's rich history.

One of the features of the new visitor center was a covered outdoor patio. This area served as a demonstration area for music and craft programs. It was also suitable for displaying some of the park's larger museum pieces, like this cannon tube. The covered patio was later enclosed.

Five

Growth and Change

This was not another park. No, this was a national historical park.

—Harry Hoe, chairman of the Cumberland Gap NHP Dedication Committee, 2008

Throughout the first few decades of the park's existence, change was the only constant. Echoing the earlier confusion of how to formally recognize the Cumberland Gap as a national park was its subsequent search for identity throughout the 1970s and 1980s. It soon became apparent that even though Cumberland Gap gained national recognition primarily for its historical connotations, many visitors came looking for more traditional park experiences. Trails, picnic areas, and a campground with amphitheater were constructed for those looking for a connection with nature.

At the same time, the rehabilitation and restoration of Cumberland Gap National Historical Park's many historical resources brought in visitors seeking a closer connection with history. Visitors also came to learn of Appalachian folkways, and the park responded by hosting old-time music performances and handicraft demonstrations. Reenactments of frontier and Civil War life proved popular, and community outreach expanded with programs teaching children about the wonders of nature.

As rehabilitation of the Hensley Settlement continued, visitation to that remote site began to rise. In the 1980s, demonstrations of sorghum-making, harvesting, and blacksmithing were great draws, and farm animals were brought in to heighten the authenticity of the scene. Oral history interviews were conducted with the former residents of the settlement in 1960 and the early 1970s, and these interviews, along with the active participation of some family members, have formed the basis of work at the site.

In response to the increased offerings at the park, visitation continued to grow, from 165,000 in 1959 to 176,000 in 1964 to close to 800,000 in 1986, and more than 900,000 in 2010.

This float depicting the new Cumberland Gap National Historical Park is making its way around the courthouse square in Pineville, Kentucky, during the annual Mountain Laurel Festival parade. The festival has been an honored Kentucky festival since 1931 and is the oldest continuous event of its kind in the country.

The opening of the Wilderness Road campground attracted visitors looking for a more traditional park experience. The ribbon cutting held in September 1957 included (from left to right) Virginia congressman Thomas B. Fugate, W.C. Asher, Hugh T. Ramsey, and Howard Douglass. As secretary of the Kentucky National Park Commission, Douglass was the principal land buyer for the park and worked tirelessly and patiently at this sometimes thankless job. (Courtesy of Tom Miles.)

The campground contained 165 campsites and was located in the Virginia side of the park, in order to create more of a balance of attractions in each state. This amphitheater was built to host ranger programs around the campfire in summer evenings, including musical performances, historical demonstrations, and reenactments. Loop trails in the campground allow campers to hike within the park without ever having to venture in to the Kentucky portion. A picnic area is located just down the road from the campground. Today, the campground includes sites with electrical hookups.

Cumberland Gap National Historical Park employees gather for a farewell cookout for Verne Ingram. This 1958 photograph was taken at the O'Dell house, the former residence of B.J. O'Dell, who owned a service station and store on the spot before the park was created. From left to right are (kneeling) Mr. Westerfield, Roy Stubbs, William Partin, and Harry Chambers; (standing) Glen Justice, Bruce Richmond, Sylvanus Harvey, Verne Ingram, Jack Caldwell, Dean Guy (superintendent), Robert Pearson, David Holmes, Hobart Cawood, and Roy Tucker. Below are the park wives at the same occasion. From left to right are Mrs. Westerfield, Mrs. Ingram, Mrs. Justice, Mrs. Cawood, Mrs. Stubbs, Mrs. Guy, Mrs. Harvey, Mrs. Partain, and Mrs. Stoddard. They formed the NPS Women's Organization for CGNHPA in 1962. Their goals were to help families of new employees adjust to the area and participate in community activities. They also took courses in first aid and fire extinguisher training and undertook a study of the Mission 66 initiative.

Installation of the tristate marker atop the ridge of Cumberland Mountain predated the establishment of the park. Here, chief ranger Lloyd Abelson (left) and historian Hobart Cawood display the state flags, from left to right, Kentucky, Virginia, and Tennessee, at the site. Below, the construction of a shelter over the marker and the addition of exhibits about each state at the corners made the point a popular destination for hikers. Near the shelter are remains of several Civil War–era fortifications.

When the park was established in 1955, the last resident of Hensley Settlement had been gone for four years, and most of the other families had left long before that. It didn't take long for Mother Nature to reclaim the old wooden structures. The Lige Gibbons farm (above) and Willie Gibbons house (below) were in advanced disrepair by the time the park was able to work on them. Although not included as part of the original enabling legislation as a resource to be preserved, the restored Hensley Settlement has consistently drawn visitors to this remote spot on top of Brush Mountain.

Before World War II, the plans had been to use the Civilian Conservation Corps (CCC) in developing the park. But the CCC was disbanded in 1942 and not until the early 1960s did Pres. Lyndon B. Johnson create the Job Corps (JC) as an employment initiative in his War on Poverty. Because Appalachia was one of the poorest regions in the nation, and as a way to expose inner-city youth to the great outdoors, a Job Corps center was established at Cumberland Gap National Historical Park. The restoration of the buildings at Hensley Settlement was one of the corps's primary jobs. Above, youth pose in front of the one of the houses with Jess Gibbons, a former resident. Gibbons helped advise the workers on the accuracy of the reconstructions. At right, park maintenance foreman Gene Miracle builds a picket fence with a JC worker.

The Job Corps worked at the park from 1964 until 1968 when Pres. Richard M. Nixon cut the funding for the program. Working on the Hensley Settlement buildings gave the youth an opportunity to work outdoors and learn skills that would not have been possible at their homes. As a result of the accurate restoration, Hensley Settlement was placed in the National Register of Historic Places in 1981.

Physical reminders of the Civil War can be found scattered around the Cumberland Gap and up the Pinnacle. Earthwork fortifications are fragile and subject to erosion from people walking on them. Here, a Job Corps group builds steps to access Fort McCook, thereby helping to protect the slopes while at the same time promoting visitor awareness of the site.

As development and investigation of the park's resources advanced, so did its collection of historic artifacts. Contractors and maintenance workers found prehistoric points and Civil War bullets and buttons, and work at Hensley uncovered items such as cooking utensils. To house these artifacts, the Job Corps built a storage room for items not on exhibit.

Along with a rigorous working schedule, the day of a Job Corps youth was also full of extracurricular activities. A new gymnasium and athletic fields provided outlets for play, and periodic dances were held to encourage the workers to mingle with the community.

As part of the park's community outreach, members of the Job Corps were assigned to community members to help them feel more at home in Middlesboro. Here, the youth participate in a parade down Cumberland Avenue in the mid-1960s.

Impromptu park ranger talks and hikes have always been popular with visitors. In this photograph, chief ranger Lloyd Abelson can be seen giving a program on the Cumberland Gap, visible from the back patio of the visitor center.

Action at the gap during the Civil War was sporadic, and during their downtime, the soldiers left signatures and other carvings on the rocks at the Pinnacle. Here, a ranger shows visitors the signature of Confederate lieutenant William R. McEntire, who was captured here in 1863. To honor McEntire's deathbed request, his grandson George visited the park in 1963, stood on this spot, and cursed the Yankees for five minutes.

In 1991, George McEntire returned to the park with his family and is shown here on the rock bearing his grandfather's signature, outlined in chalk.

Although surrounded by the new national park, Cudjo's Cave continued to be operated by LMU until 1992. Below, a ranger gazes at Hercules Column, while crystal-clear Cleopatra's Pool, seen at left, was a favorite place for dreamers to throw their pennies and make a wish.

Sand Cave, one of the more spectacular spots in the Virginia side of the park, is located along the Ridge Trail. In this photograph by Earl Palmer, the lone occupant is dwarfed by the soaring ceiling and vast sand floor of the rock shelter.

Here, a ranger interacts with a group at the Pinnacle Overlook in the 1970s. There's always plenty to show and talk about there, with views into Kentucky, Tennessee, and Virginia. Fern Lake can be seen in the center right of the photograph.

Cumberland Gap played an important role in many periods of American history. The primary theme of the park is the era of the pioneer and the Wilderness Road, as illustrated in this early sign, but the area's Civil War history is also commemorated through events and reenactments.

Living history presentations have always been a staple of national park programs, and firing guns and artillery pieces is popular with visitors. Demonstrating the long-hunter rifle takes training in black powder and special safety precautions, but serves to convey the reality of life on the frontier as few other programs can.

Firing the cannon and drilling with young visitors were part of the standard Civil War interpretive activities in the 1980s. Of all the historic time periods presented at the park, the Civil War era is of particular interest, partially because of the significant resources still extant on the Pinnacle and up the Tri-State Peak. Recent scholarship and archeological surveys have uncovered more Civil War–era sites within the park than were previously known. A focus in the national parks on the 150th anniversary of the war has also attracted more visitors interested in that era of American history at Cumberland Gap.

The Sugar Run Day Camp was offered for two summers at Cumberland Gap National Historical Park in the 1970s. In an effort to engage local youth with the natural resources of the park, rangers took them on hikes and played outdoor games. Above, ranger Lee Wilder leads a group around the Hensley Settlement; below, rangers Goodwin and Miller lead the campers in a game called the web of life. Today, schools regularly bring their students on field trips and picnics to the park.

Musical programs and demonstrations at the park tend to focus on the traditional Appalachian instruments and songs. Here, a costumed ranger is demonstrating the dulcimer to a group of children during the Sugar Run Day Camp. The park hosts a dulcimer convention each spring at the Wilderness Road campground.

For a few years in the 1970s, the park participated in annual bird counts. Rangers Steve Beatty and Cindy Nicholson lead a bird hike along the Ridge Trail near Hensley Settlement. Guided hikes focusing on topics as varied as wildflowers, owls, and photography are still offered throughout the year.

The relationship between national parks and the Boy Scouts of America is a long and proud one, and at Cumberland Gap, the Scout heritage as the Sons of Daniel Boone has added meaning. Several Scouts have earned their Eagle Scout ranks by working on park-related projects. Above, in a photograph from 1963, the Flaming Arrow Patrol from Harlan pauses for a break by Gap Creek at the iron furnace before their hike. Below, a Scout troop gets a lesson in building a campfire ring at the backcountry campsite at Martin's Fork near Hensley Settlement.

The Mischa Mokwa Trail was founded in 1966 by the Scouts and Explorers of Middlesboro, Kentucky, a precursor to Troop No. 544. In the above photograph, members of the troop pose with chief ranger Lloyd Abelson at the new trailhead. The trail is a 19-mile-long walk along the ridgetop that takes scouts through Hensley and past the Sand Cave and White Rocks. It has remained relatively unchanged over the years and was built to provide scouts a true wilderness adventure. At right, members of Troop No. 544 bike the Boone Trail, a new trail that links the Harrogate greenway and the Ewing Rails to Trails routes.

After the Job Corps and, later, the Youth Conservation Corps, restored the buildings at Hensley Settlement, it was used as a living history farm for much of the late 1970s and 1980s. Farm animals were brought in to live at the farm, and demonstrations of plowing and harvesting wheat were given on a regular basis. Above, park employee Chester Thomas works the fields and, below, volunteers load cane for use in making sorghum. Today, tours of the settlement are available seasonally, with the only vehicular access by park van.

Another old-time traditional activity celebrated at the restored settlement was that of making moonshine. Although the subject has sometimes been controversial, information in the oral history interviews done with residents back in 1960 and 1970 indicate that some family members did make—and in some instances, sell—moonshine.

The annual Hensley and Gibbons family reunion, seen here in 1968, brings hundreds of family and friends to the settlement in August. At this time, they tour the restored buildings, decorate the graves, and share their memories of life on the mountain with visitors and rangers. It's also one of the few days per year that visitors are allowed to drive their own vehicles up the narrow and steep Shillalah Creek Road.

In this photograph from 1979, several park employees can be seen moving a Parrott gun into place at Fort Lyon, a well-preserved Civil War earthwork located atop the Pinnacle. Although none of the three cannons on display in the park were originally used at Cumberland Gap, they are all authentic artifacts and are protected as such.

The amphitheater at the campground is the site of weekend programs during the summer months, offering everything from music performances to pioneer demonstrations. Interpretive ranger Linda Stanton gives a campfire program about Appalachian traditions in the home during an evening program in 1969.

A blacksmithing demonstration at the amphitheater in 1975 shows visitors some of the skills employed by Willie Gibbons at the settlement. The Saturday evening programs are a good way for visitors to learn more about the park and area if they are just staying a short time.

Natural disasters can wreak havoc even in natural areas. A 1977 flood caused this landslide of rocks down the Shillalah Creek road leading to Hensley Settlement. Maintenance employee Gene Miracle stands ankle deep in debris. Sometimes, a disaster can have an unexpected result: a landslide caused by torrential rains in 2011 uncovered an unknown Civil War campsite.

In the tradition of the CCC and the Job Corps, the Youth Conservation Corps worked at the park in the 1970s, helping with trail building and rail fencing, as shown here. The national parks have long partnered with youth service groups, including today's AmeriCorps and Student Conservation Association (SCA).

Six

Coming Full Circle

The opening of a new chapter in American frontier history.

—Dr. Thomas Clark, *My Century in History*

Today, visitors to the Cumberland Gap National Historical Park can safely drive through a state-of-the-art tunnel under the mountain, park their cars, and walk along the rehabilitated Wilderness Road. This simple experience was decades in the making.

Not too long ago, it seemed that the success of the Cumberland Gap was leading to its demise. The paved road through the gap that signaled such progress in the 1920s had earned the Cumberland Gap another nickname, "Massacre Mountain," because of the many accidents that occurred each year. Once again, hundreds of thousands of people were crossing the gap, but many didn't even realize the significance of their passage.

Since the early days of the park's existence, the idea had been floated to somehow remove some, if not all, of the traffic from the highway over the mountain. Not until the 1970s, however, did the dream begin to take shape, as park attention returned to the problem of US Highway 25E.

The proposed solution of a tunnel under the mountain for vehicle traffic would prove to be the first step needed to bring the Cumberland Gap back almost full circle to its 19th-century state. This construction and the subsequent restoration of the trail through the gap were the most ambitious projects of their kind in the National Park Service.

The last two decades of the Cumberland Gap National Historical Park have seen the greatest changes in its existence. Unusual in its mission of not only preserving history but actually turning back the clock on its landscape, the park has become a magnet for genealogists, those who want to follow their ancestors in that westward journey to a new life. It is said that more than 48 million Americans can trace their forefathers as having traveled through the Cumberland Gap. Today, their descendants can do the same.

As traffic increased over the Cumberland Gap, so did accidents. Car wrecks over the old Highway 25E through the Gap were frequent and sometimes deadly. The two-lane winding road had steep drop-offs at times, and that combined with the excessive speed of many to create its nickname of Massacre Mountain. Note the "Welcome to Kentucky" sign on the shoulder of the road in the image above.

The national park had jurisdiction over the stretch of highway that bisected the park, so rangers were often called out to investigate the accidents. Not all accidents involved other motorists; some were acts of nature, as seen in this 1962 photograph of a tree down on the highway.

This snowy view of the town of Cumberland Gap from the Pinnacle Overlook shows the area before the tunnel was built. The winding road in the center of the image is US Highway 25E making its way through the town of Cumberland Gap before crossing the mountain. When the highway was rerouted as a result of the construction in the 1990s, it no longer ran through the town, a change welcomed by some residents and lamented by others.

When the legislation was signed in 1973 for the building of a tunnel under the Cumberland Gap, funding did not automatically follow. This pilot tunnel wasn't built until 1985, twelve years after the project was approved. Temporary tracks were laid to enable the carrying of materials to and from the construction site.

The vast amount of road work required by the building of the tunnels can be seen in this photograph from 1992, taken from the Tennessee side of the Cumberland Mountain. The southbound tunnel (left) was completed before the northbound one into Kentucky.

This is a photograph of the interior of one of the bores of the tunnel during construction. When the tunnel was built, it was discovered that the mountain has a number of natural caves with prolific springs and a lake 30 feet deep, which required lining the tunnel with a waterproof PVC membrane. Daily water quality monitoring was conducted during the building of the tunnel.

Diverting traffic away from the saddle of the Cumberland Gap to the new tunnels required the rerouting of two highways. Approximately 1.25 miles of Virginia Highway 58 was rerouted to merge with US Highway 25E south of the gap. This photograph shows the phenomenon of the "fogfall," when fog trapped in the meteorite crater of Middlesboro escapes through the gap.

The opening of the Cumberland Gap Tunnel attracted many dignitaries, including the governors and congressmen of all three states. The keynote speaker was the US representative from Kentucky, Hal Rogers (in the white coat). Next to Rogers, from left to right, are Kentucky governor Paul Patton, Tennessee governor Don Sundquist, and Virginia governor George Allen. In the back row are Jerry Belson of the NPS (left) and Mayor Ben Hickman (with his hat over his heart) of Middlesboro, Kentucky.

The grand opening of the tunnel was quite a production. Visitors braved a rainy day in October 1996 to listen to the governors of the three states and other dignitaries dedicate the new road under the mountain. Since the tunnels were built, traffic through the gap has increased to an average of 11 million cars per year.

When the speeches were finished, the program began. One of the more dramatic scenes was the procession of historical reenactors that walked through the tunnel. The long hunters (above) appear from the tunnel in a mist, helped along by the foggy, damp day. Other reenactors in the procession included Native Americans, antique cars, and Civil War soldiers. Bringing up the rear of this parade of history was Boy Scout Troop No. 544, heralding the future of the Cumberland Gap. Holding the banner below are, from left to right, Jeremy Metcalf, Michael Hawk, and Brad Wilder.

Because of the historic nature of the park, law mandates that the park does extensive research and surveying before undergoing any major ground-disturbing work. Consequently, a thorough archeological investigation was undertaken prior to the restoration of the Wilderness Road. Here, park ranger Jimmy Johnson stands beside an old stone wall uncovered during this survey work. Prehistoric and historic resources were preserved during the restoration.

Infrastructure was necessary to support the new walking trail created by the restoration. A visitor information center was built at the Virginia trailhead of the Wilderness Road. Besides restrooms and a kiosk, the visitor information center features metal sculptures representing the many travelers through the gap over the centuries. As hikers walk by the figures, they can hear the sounds of a wagon train passing by.

Throughout the dizzying changes of the 20th century, the 1915 DAR monument remained one of the few constant presences at the saddle of the gap. Local historian James Schenkenfelder brought the neglected condition of the monument to the attention of the park, and with help from the four state DAR chapters, the monument was repaired and rededicated in June 2004. On hand for the ceremony was Daniel Boone himself, as portrayed by Scott New.

This 2001 view down the Wilderness Road would have been impossible just two years before. Here, construction vehicles travel down toward the Kentucky side of the gap. Indian Rock is located just beyond the bank of earth on the left. The Skyland Road can be seen in the distance.

When the park acquired Cudjo's Cave from Lincoln Memorial University in 1992, the cave was closed for renovations to restore it to its historic appearance. Part of the work included removing modern intrusions such as recent graffiti, lighting, and artificially created features, as seen here. In 2000, the cave was reopened as Gap Cave, the name given it by Dr. Thomas Walker in 1750.

The restored Wilderness Road was dedicated on October 19, 2002, almost exactly six years after the opening of the tunnels. Dr. Thomas Clark, state historian for Kentucky, observed that the park had "set in juxtaposition . . . the modern age of America [and] a primitive trail that was the path of American civilization itself." US representative Hal Rogers from Kentucky joined the reenactors as they walked the trail.

Since the restoration of the Wilderness Road, significant historical events have been recreated upon it, including a dramatic procession of the descendants of those who traveled the road west 200 years ago. Here, Lewis and Clark reenactors make an appearance in the saddle of the gap on the bicentennial of their trip through the Cumberland Gap in 2006, while a park ranger watches from above.

The opening of the tunnel under Cumberland Mountain heralded an increase in traffic through the national park. Approximately 11 million vehicles drive through the tunnel annually, although only a fraction take the time to visit the park. Tourist or not, anyone driving through the park is subject to federal laws and regulations, and is likely to be stopped by a park ranger if caught speeding.

With the removal of the highway and the restoration of a continuous landscape, wildlife not seen in the area in decades has found its way back to Cumberland Gap. Here, researchers and park staff attach a tracking collar to a bear that has been sedated in order to learn whether there is a den with cubs in the park.

With the arrival of several invasive species like the hemlock woolly adelgid (HWA), the park's resource management division uses the latest techniques to try to combat diseases that attack both flora and fauna. Here, an SCA worker treats a hemlock tree with an injection to kill the HWA and try to prevent further infestation.

On July 4, 2009, Cumberland Gap National Historical Park celebrated the 50th anniversary of its dedication. Several events from the 1959 ceremony were duplicated, including the Nation's First Parade of the 49 State Flags. Above, Supt. Mark Woods addresses the crowd at the anniversary celebration. Next to him are, from left to right, LMU trustee Gary Burchett; John Brown, chairman of the new Friends of Cumberland Gap organization; Virginia Huff, one of the first employees of the park; and Harry Hoe, chairman of the original 1959 dedication committee. Below, leading Boy Scout Troop No. 544 is volunteer Albert Earle, who also led the 1959 parade as a Boy Scout of 13 years old. (Above, courtesy of Harold Jerrell.)

More than a decade has passed since the restoration of the Wilderness Road through the Cumberland Gap. The vegetation has grown lush in the Appalachian rain, and during the summer months, all traces of the old highway vanish. On any given day, hikers can be seen making their way across the mountain, once again able to experience the wonders of America's first frontier. (Courtesy of Scott Teodorski.)

Bibliography

Earle, David R. "When Science Came to the Wilderness, the Story of Camp Harvard," *Gateway*, The Journal of the Bell County Historical Society, Spring 2013: 7–13.
Jones, Randell. *Trailing Daniel Boone*. Winston-Salem, NC: Daniel Boone Footsteps, 2012.
Kincaid, Robert. *The Wilderness Road*. Indianapolis: Bobbs-Merrill Company, 1947.
Luckett, William W. "Cumberland Gap National Historical Park," *Tennessee Historical Quarterly*. Tennessee Historical Society, December 1964, Vol. XXIII, No. 4.
Matheny, Ann. *The Magic City*. Middlesboro, KY: Bell County Historical Society, 2003.
Speer, Jean Haskell. *The Appalachian Photographs of Earl Palmer*. Lexington, Kentucky: University Press of Kentucky, 1990.
Tinney, Edward E. *History of Cumberland Gap National Historical Park*, US Department of the Interior, 1965.
Ward, Neil. "Marsee Chapel," *Gateway*, Winter 2012: 3–7.
Woods, Mark. "An Appalachian Tale; Restoring Boone's Wilderness Road," *CRM No. 5*, 2002: 20–22.

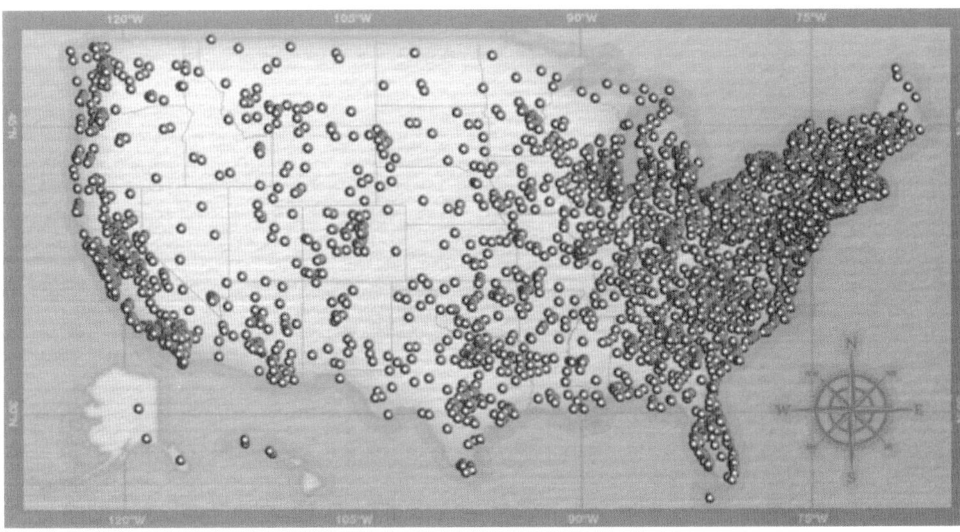